Bake the Seasons

Bake the Seasons

Sweet and Savoury
Dishes to Enjoy
Throughout the Year

Marcella DiLonardo

PENGUIN

an imprint of Penguin Canada, a division of Penguin Random House Canada Limited

Canada • USA • UK • Ireland • Australia • New Zealand • India • South Africa • China

First published 2019

www.penguinrandomhouse.ca

LIBRARY AND ARCHIVES CANADA CATALOGUING IN PUBLICATION

DiLonardo, Marcella, author
      Bake the seasons : sweet and savoury dishes to enjoy
throughout the year / Marcella DiLonardo.

Includes index.
Issued also in print and electronic formats.
ISBN 978-0-7352-3519-9 (softcover).—ISBN 978-0-7352-3520-5 (electronic)

      1. Baking. 2. Seasonal cooking. 3. Cookbooks. I. Title.

TX763.D55 2019   641.81'5   C2018-904241-9
                                          C2018-904242-7

Cover and interior design by Jennifer Griffiths
Cover images and interior photography by Marcella DiLonardo

Printed and bound in China

10 9 8 7 6 5 4 3 2 1

Penguin
Random House
PENGUIN CANADA

To Justin.

You are the Jeffrey to my Ina.

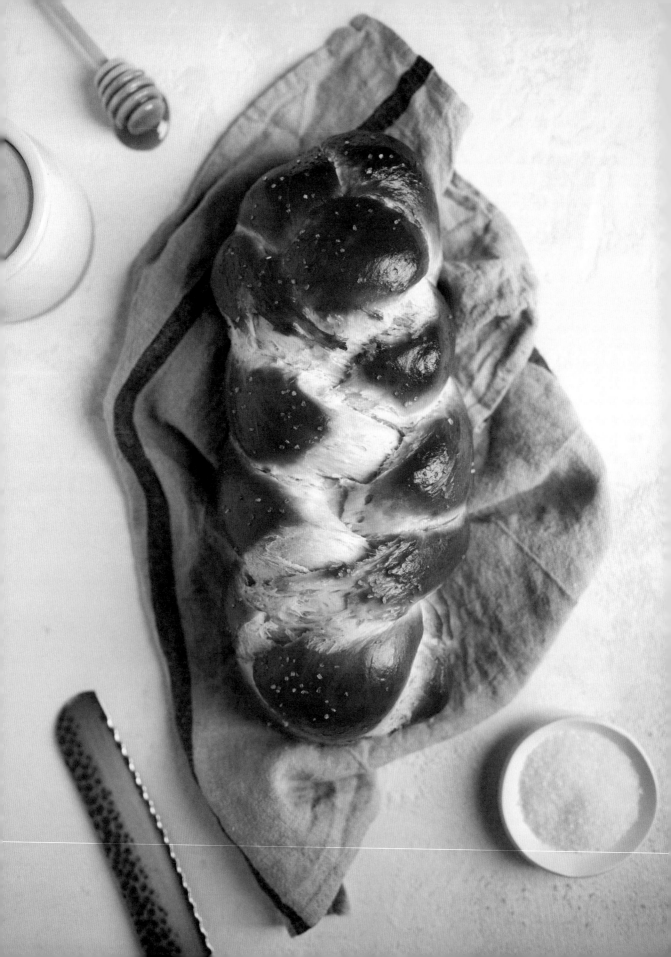

Contents

Introduction

EVER SINCE I was sixteen, I would tell anyone who'd listen that one day I would write a cookbook. Though I said this often, a big part of me never actually expected it to happen. After I graduated from university, I moved to downtown Toronto with high hopes and big dreams of a career in media, but ended up working at the Eaton Centre for minimum wage. If you had told me back then that today I would have my own lifestyle blog and be sharing my recipes with the world, I would have called you crazy and returned to folding underwear at my retail job.

I spent my nights baking and my days off exploring the city, spending every cent I could spare at the latest trendy restaurants. It wasn't long after moving to Toronto that I met Justin. On our third date, I made us dinner, and he brought banana bread for dessert. A slight miscalculation had resulted in Justin doubling the required amount of butter—this was a man after my own heart! My lonely nights of baking were soon replaced with Food Network binge-watching with Justin over a plate of freshly baked chocolate chip cookies. But my baking journey started long before Justin, with many turns and detours. Let's go back to the beginning . . .

Growing up in a traditional Italian family meant spending hours in the kitchen with my mom and grandmothers. From an early age, I played with pasta dough instead of Play-Doh. My grandmothers were happy to take advantage of my tiny thumbs and kept me busy rolling tray after tray of cavatelli and gnocchi, and before long, I was rolling out fresh pasta dough with a hand crank from the 1960s. We also spent lots of time outdoors, picking strawberries at neighbouring farms (although, honestly, more of them made their way into my mouth than into the basket) and canning a summer's worth of peaches and tomatoes from our garden. As I got older, and my overprotective grandmothers finally allowed me to use the stove and oven, I fell in love with baking. Of course I wanted to learn my grandmothers' cherished recipes. However, as you may know, Italians take their recipes to the grave. I remember one day helping one grandmother to make her famous braciole, and she sent me to get more flour. When I returned, I saw that several more ingredients had been added to the mixing bowl, and when I asked what they were, she told me, "Don't worry about it."

So I learned the basics from my grandmothers, but I also knew that I would have to create recipes of my own. The main lesson I took away from my years spent in the kitchen with my mom and grandmothers was how to make simple dishes with fresh, seasonal, local ingredients. No two ways about it, fresh produce tastes best when it's in season. Bonus points if it was grown right in your own backyard. When fruits and vegetables are at their best, they are the star ingredients in any dish.

When I headed off to university, I quickly found myself daydreaming about recipes when I should have been paying attention to my economics professors. My sister was in her third year, which meant her dorm had a kitchen, so a few times a week I would go to her place and bake cakes, cookies and other tasty goods while she studied. While my friends went out to bars and clubs on the weekends, I was watching the Food Network—Bobby Flay, Ina Garten, Michael Smith, Giada De Laurentiis, Anna Olson—I couldn't get enough. I admired Bobby's love for grilling and using blue corn in just about everything, Giada's spin on the Italian dishes I grew up eating, Ina's . . . well, I love everything about Ina Garten. Her confidence in the kitchen and her classic approach to cooking mixed with her enthusiasm for quality ingredients captured everything I wanted to be. When I discovered that Anna Olson lived just around the corner from where I grew up, I felt a flicker of hope: if she could do it, maybe one day I could too. But I didn't want to just mimic recipes I had seen on TV; I wanted to create my own, with the same finesse as the chefs on the Food Network. (Except for Ina—no one can compete with the Barefoot Contessa.)

I was always excited to return home to help prepare our annual Christmas dinner, and I begged my mom to let me help with the cooking—I didn't want to just wash fruit and peel potatoes. No surprise, Mom was reluctant to give up her reigning title as the best cook in the family, but after much back-and-forthing, we came to an agreement: she would cook and I would bake. And so began a new tradition. While the first few years were a little rocky (there was a pumpkin pie fiasco I will never live down), the more I baked, the better I became. Through trial and error, practice indeed made perfect. Each year I would come up with an even fancier and better dessert than the year before. What started as Christmas baking turned into baking cakes for every family occasion.

I will always love baking for my family, yet what I really wanted was to make a career of it, and in 2013, Justin finally persuaded me to start a food blog. He wanted me to share with the world what makes me happy and what I do best. I never expected

anyone to read my blog—other than my family and friends—but I dreamed that recipe developing would one day become my full-time job. I knew that success in this field would take hard work, but at the very least, having a blog would provide me with the creative outlet I desperately needed and would be the perfect place to document my latest kitchen triumphs.

The more recipes I created for my blog, the more I improved as a baker and recipe developer. I began breaking out of my comfort zone, working with ingredients and flavour combinations I would never have thought to try before. I developed my own style by modernizing rustic dishes, making these not-so-beautiful desserts beautiful. As the months passed and my blog following grew, not only did the cooking and baking motivate me, but I began to fall in love with the photography side of things. I could see how my photography was bringing my recipes alive and enticing people to bake alongside me, and so I taught myself everything I could about this second form of art.

As the years passed, I found myself growing tired of city life. I dreamed of cooking on my own Lacanche range, and that was never going to happen in a one-bedroom condo with the tiniest nook of a kitchen. My kitchen cupboards were overflowing with supplies, so much so that I was keeping things in the spare tub! I knew it was time for a bigger place—somewhere Justin and I could settle down with our family (of dogs). We found our dream house in the small town of Fonthill, and traded in our subway passes for a compact car. I don't have the kind of backyard garden my grandparents relied on for their produce, but I'm lucky enough to be surrounded by the endless farms and orchards of the Niagara region, as well to have a mom who drops off a weekly supply of fresh herbs, tomatoes, zucchini and peppers throughout the summer.

Not everyone is lucky enough to have an orchard steps away from their front door, so I recommend exploring farmers' markets and supermarkets for locally grown produce. These flavours constantly inspire me, so much so that *Bake the Seasons* was born from that passion. Each chapter in this book explores how to bake with fresh, seasonal produce, as I let you in on my favourite sweet and savoury baking recipes for breakfast, lunch, dinner and dessert. I have even included my favourite baked comfort dishes, like Roasted Butternut Squash Mac and Cheese (page 171), because when it comes to baking, I don't believe in limiting myself to just a traditional dough or batter.

Baking with seasonal and local ingredients works to the advantage of a home baker for a variety of reasons. Not only does in-season produce provide better flavour in a recipe, but it will be readily available at local grocery stores and farmers' markets. There is nothing enjoyable about spending double the price on sour strawberries in the fall. And have you ever tried to make a peach pie in the winter? Let me tell you, I didn't know a peach could be so dry. When a season like winter lacks produce, you'll find that my sweet baking relies more heavily on the flavours of the season—like eggnog, spices and candy cane—and my savoury dishes centre around hearty greens, root vegetables and bread baking.

The recipes in this book may be arranged by season, but I encourage you to experiment with substituting one season's produce for another. The Rhubarb Oat Squares (page 21) can be switched up in the summer with peach compote instead of rhubarb, and in the fall by using homemade pumpkin butter or apple butter. Dishes like Cherry Almond Dutch Baby (page 39) and Apricot Raspberry Clafoutis (page 84) will work beautifully with any sweet fruit you can get your hands on. The recipes for my baked goods are simple and involve only a handful of ingredients, so treat them as base recipes for whatever you dream up throughout the year.

The simplicity of the recipes in *Bake the Seasons* reflects the simple style of baking I blog about each week. I want home bakers to be able to recreate these dishes without having to run to the store to purchase a long list of ingredients. While a few showstopper recipes do require a little extra love and elbow grease, and are perfect for special occasions, on the whole I like my everyday baked goods simple. Many recipes in this book are easy enough to whip up on a weeknight or on a relaxed Sunday morning when a brunch craving strikes.

I hope you'll find inspiration within these pages, and that you'll find yourself switching on your oven all year round, whether you need a quick party appetizer in the winter (try my Roasted Garlic and Cheese Pull-Apart Bread, page 213), a flavourful addition to a neighbourhood potluck in the summer (I can't speak highly enough of my Jalapeño Cheddar Cornbread, page 112), an Easter dessert for a crowd in the spring (my Maple Carrot Cake on page 25 is the perfect option) or a new, flavourful breakfast option to kick off the fall (you can't go wrong with my Pumpkin Pie Granola, page 123). There really is nothing more satisfying and comforting than baking throughout the seasons.

Stocked Pantry

THE MAJORITY OF recipes in *Bake the Seasons* focus on seasonal flavours, many with fresh produce at the heart. I love tailoring my baking and cooking to what I can find at my local farmers' market, and you'll notice that my recipes don't rely on lots of fancy ingredients. Still, there are a number of staples that every home baker should keep on hand at all times. A well-stocked pantry ensures that you'll never run out of key ingredients, and when a craving strikes, you can whip up something amazing without having to run to the store.

I recommend baking with quality ingredients, as the superior end result is always worth that little bit extra you might spend. My baking philosophy has always focused on quality over quantity and allowing each ingredient to shine through. Below you'll find the staples that I always keep on hand in my pantry and refrigerator.

FLOUR

There are so many brands of flour available in grocery stores, how do you choose? I recommend spending a little more money on higher-quality flour, especially in any recipe where it's the main ingredient, like bread. I tested all my recipes with Bob's Red Mill unbleached white all-purpose flour, which is my go-to flour. It is certified organic, grown in North America and not enriched with any fillers or additives. You can find this flour in most supermarkets or purchase it online from Bob's Red Mill, although any quality unbleached all-purpose flour will work in my recipes. It is important not to substitute pastry flour or bread flour, as both have a different protein content, which will change the texture of your baked goods. Get in the habit of sifting the flour before each use, as sifting will give you a more accurate measurement and eliminate the inconsistencies across brands due to some flours being packed denser than others.

SUGAR

The majority of my sweet recipes call for turbinado sugar. This raw sugar is more natural than granulated sugar, plus I love the crystal crunch and caramel colouring it brings to my baking. (It is important not to confuse raw sugar with brown sugar. Brown sugar is just granulated sugar mixed with molasses.) I recommend keeping granulated sugar, light brown sugar and icing sugar on hand too. I use granulated sugar when turbinado sugar would be too coarse for more delicate baked goods. I always reach for icing sugar when making frostings, as it is ground into a fine powder that ensures it dissolves easily into the butter as it whips. And some of my recipes work best with light brown sugar.

EGGS

The recipes in this book were tested using large eggs, and I recommend sticking to this size to ensure consistency in the structure and texture of your baked goods. I am lucky enough to be surrounded by farms where I live, and I go to the market once a week to pick up fresh eggs. If you don't have access to a farm or weekly farmers' market, free-range eggs are readily available at chain supermarkets.

BUTTER

I use unsalted butter in my baking. Butter is one of the foundational ingredients in baking, providing a rich flavour like no other. Any brand of unsalted butter will work, but higher-quality butter with an 80% fat content will provide the best flavour. Read the labels carefully, though. Butters with a higher fat content, closer to 85%, will melt faster, altering the final texture of a baked good.

Using unsalted butter also allows me to control the amount of salt in each dish, which ensures a recipe will turn out the same every time.

Note that some recipes call for cold butter and others for room-temperature butter. Cold butter is needed when making things like pie dough and biscuits, as it yields a much flakier texture, whereas butter needs to be at room temperature to ensure proper creaming with sugar, an important step in cake and cookie recipes.

MILK

For all my baking I use whole milk (at least 3.25%). I prefer the flavour that the higher fat content brings. Lower-fat milks have a higher ratio of water, so they don't, as you might guess, provide as much flavour to your baking.

CREAM

I love the richness and flavour that cream brings to a dish. I stick to heavy, a.k.a. whipping, cream (about 35%), as I find it provides delicious creaminess in savoury fillings,

like in my Spinach and Chard Gratin (page 56). Do not substitute lighter creams or milk for heavy cream. The swap will result in an unfavourable consistency change, not to mention the loss of that rich flavour.

OILS

For baking, I prefer neutral-flavoured oils such as canola or vegetable oil. These can be used interchangeably and add moisture to baked goods, like my Ultimate Banana Bread (page 148). For savoury baking, the Italian in me uses high-quality extra-virgin olive oil (not to be confused with regular olive oil). Extra-virgin olive oil adds fresh, bold flavour to savoury baking, which you'll notice in dishes like my Winter Pear and Smoked Gorgonzola Pizza (page 209). I love dipping fresh-baked bread into this oil and then sprinkling it with a pinch of salt. Try that with my No-Knead Olive Rosemary Bread (page 115)!

VINEGAR

I keep a variety of vinegars on hand, including white vinegar, rice vinegar and apple cider vinegar, but the one I use most is balsamic vinegar. I recommend using a high-quality balsamic vinegar, such as balsamic imported from Italy. It provides an intense flavour and is more concentrated than a lower-quality version.

BAKING POWDER

Baking powder is a mix of baking soda, cream of tartar and cornstarch, and it provides leavening to biscuits and cakes. In the majority of my recipes, the ratio of baking powder to flour is 1 teaspoon (5 mL) powder for every cup (250 mL) of flour. Just like spices, it does lose its potency over time, so be sure to keep an eye on its expiration date. Most home bakers need to replace it before finishing the container.

BAKING SODA

Baking soda and baking powder are not interchangeable in a recipe. They are both leavening agents but they work very differently, so be sure to use the one your recipe calls for.

YEAST

I always have ¼-ounce (8 g) packets of instant yeast—also labelled quick-rise—on hand in my pantry. Rather than purchasing a large jar and risking it going bad, purchasing smaller portions helps ensure freshness. I've had the most success using instant yeast in my bread-baking adventures and find it much easier to work with than active dry yeast, as it doesn't need to be dissolved in liquid first. However, instant yeast and active dry yeast are interchangeable in the recipes in this book. To test whether your yeast is still active, stir it into some warm water. If it isn't foamy after about five minutes, start over with new yeast.

SALT

You'll notice that many of the recipes in *Bake the Seasons* call for fine salt. By this I mean fine table salt, which is ground very finely to ensure it breaks down during cooking and baking. I also keep coarse salt on hand for baking salted desserts, breads and pretzels. It has a weaker salt taste by volume, but the large crystals give the perfect salty bite. I recommend using the amount of salt specified in a recipe, because salt plays such an important role in both sweet baking and savoury: it balances out the sugar, enhances the texture of baked goods, and enhances and brings together the flavours of the other ingredients.

VANILLA

It's rare I bake a dessert that doesn't include a splash of vanilla. Because it's such a key ingredient, I recommend purchasing quality pure vanilla extract. It's best to go for the real deal—artificial vanilla extracts will alter the taste of a recipe.

SPICES

The three spices I use most are cinnamon, ginger and nutmeg. In the fall and winter months, spices are my jam. I sprinkle cinnamon on just about everything, even my morning coffee. It provides an instant cozy feel. In the winter I also love to use allspice and cloves, but I purchase these in smaller quantities to prevent waste. Label your spices with their purchase date, as they gradually lose their vibrant flavour and should be replaced at least once a year.

NUTS

I love baking with raw pecans and walnuts. These can be used interchangeably, depending on your mood or what you have on hand. I buy my nuts in small quantities, and from a store with high turnover, to ensure they are always fresh when I need them. Any leftovers are best stored in airtight containers at room temperature for up to six months, or they can be frozen in a sealed freezer bag for up to a year.

HERBS

I use a lot of fresh herbs in my cooking. They provide freshness and vibrancy to my recipes. I'm lucky to have room to grow herbs in my garden during the spring and summer and on my windowsills in the colder months. I also dry bunches of thyme, oregano

and rosemary to use throughout the winter. Although I prefer to bake with fresh herbs, Simply Organics offers a range of quality dried herbs that are nice to have in the pantry as a backup.

CHOCOLATE

I am part of a chocolate-loving family, so I always have milk chocolate, dark chocolate and white chocolate in my pantry. Chocolate has a long shelf life—up to a year when stored at room temperature—but it's safe to say I've never had any around long enough to go bad. The recipes in *Bake the Seasons* were tested using Ghirardelli baking bars, and when it comes to dark chocolate, I use 60% cacao bittersweet chocolate. Baking with a high-quality chocolate will yield the best baked goods, as lower-quality chocolate often contains a lot of added sugar and fillers to mimic better chocolate. Instead of using chocolate chips in my cookies, I always use chunks. There is something so rustic and beautiful about imperfect pieces of chopped chocolate.

COCOA POWDER

I recommend keeping Dutch-processed cocoa powder in your pantry. This type of cocoa powder has been treated with alkali, which mellows the cocoa's natural acidity. It features a darker colour and a richer chocolate flavour in comparison to natural cocoa. As with any ingredient, choose a quality brand such as Valrhona.

Spring

I LOVE that feeling of coming out of hibernation in the spring, when you start picking up local produce at your farmers' market again. It's a transition from comfort foods to fresh spring dishes.

In this section you'll find recipes featuring asparagus, rhubarb and spinach, to name a few. One of my favourite vegetables is asparagus, which I've baked into my Asparagus Balsamic Tart (page 49) and the Asparagus, Prosciutto and Wild Mushroom Frittata (page 40). I can't get enough of these green spears! A less familiar but equally wonderful item is garlic scapes. I get extra excited when they pop up at the market, not only because this means the best locally grown garlic is just around the corner, but also because I love using garlic scapes in stir-fries, on pizza and in savoury baked goods like my Garlic Scape Brie Biscuits (page 61). One of the most iconic flavours of the season is the wonderful tartness of rhubarb. I've included a baking classic with my Strawberry Rhubarb Pie (page 27) and expanded on my rhubarb repertoire with Rhubarb Oat Squares (page 21) and Cherry Rhubarb Cobbler (page 36), which is perfect in the late spring when the first sweet cherries arrive at the market.

Hummingbird Cupcakes

This was the recipe I became known for among friends and family before starting my blog. Hummingbird cake, which hails from the southern U.S., was unknown where I grew up, so when I first made it for company, the flavour combination wowed everyone. Reminiscent of both carrot cake and banana bread, hummingbird cake includes pineapple, banana and warm spices and is topped with a thick cream cheese frosting. It's not hard to understand why these cupcakes are a real crowd-pleaser!

1. Preheat the oven to 325°F (160°C). Line 2 cupcake tins with 24 cupcake liners.

2. In a large mixing bowl sift together the flour, baking soda, salt, cinnamon and nutmeg.

3. In a separate large mixing bowl whisk together the eggs, sugar, oil and vanilla until fluffy, about 2 minutes. Stir in the bananas, pineapple, coconut and pecans. Add the flour mixture to the wet ingredients and beat until smooth, about 2 minutes.

4. Divide the mixture evenly among the cupcake liners. Bake for 20 to 25 minutes, until the tops bounce back when touched or a toothpick inserted in the centre comes out clean. Let cool on a rack while you prepare the Cream Cheese Frosting.

5. Transfer the frosting to a large pastry bag fitted with a large open star tip. Holding the bag vertically above a cupcake, squeeze while moving in a circular motion. Once you reach the top, about 2 inches (5 cm) high, stop squeezing and gently lift off. Repeat with the remaining cupcakes.

BAKER'S NOTE I made this recipe into cupcakes because I like the option of topping them mile high with frosting, but this recipe also makes a great layer cake. Simply follow the instructions for the Maple Carrot Cake (page 25) to make a three-layer 8-inch (20 cm) round cake. Bake for 25 minutes, or until a toothpick inserted in the centre comes out clean, let cool, then frost as directed.

MAKES: *24 cupcakes*

PREP TIME: *20 minutes*

COOK TIME: *20 minutes*

3 cups (750 mL) all-purpose flour

1½ teaspoons (7 mL) baking soda

1 teaspoon (5 mL) fine salt

1 teaspoon (5 mL) cinnamon

¼ teaspoon (1 mL) nutmeg

3 large eggs

2½ cups (625 mL) turbinado sugar

1¼ cups (300 mL) canola oil

2 teaspoons (10 mL) pure vanilla extract

4 very ripe bananas, mashed

1 cup (250 mL) canned crushed pineapple, drained

¾ cup (175 mL) unsweetened shredded coconut

¾ cup (175 mL) pecans, roughly chopped

1 batch Cream Cheese Frosting (page 239)

Roasted Strawberry Oat Muffins

MAKES: *12 muffins*

PREP TIME: *15 minutes*

COOK TIME: *40 minutes*

ROASTED STRAWBERRIES

2 cups (500 mL) halved
  strawberries

1 tablespoon (15 mL) pure maple
  syrup

1 teaspoon (5 mL) pure vanilla
  extract

MUFFINS

1 cup (250 mL) plain or vanilla
  full-fat yogurt

½ cup (125 mL) turbinado sugar,
  plus more for sprinkling

½ cup (125 mL) canola oil

¼ cup (60 mL) pure maple syrup

1 teaspoon (5 mL) pure vanilla
  extract

1 large egg

1 cup (250 mL) all-purpose flour

1 teaspoon (5 mL) baking soda

½ teaspoon (2 mL) baking
  powder

½ teaspoon (2 mL) fine salt

1 cup (250 mL) old-fashioned
  rolled oats, plus more for
  sprinkling

Roasting strawberries is the perfect way to boost their flavour and sweetness; tossing them in a splash of maple syrup boosts that flavour and sweetness even more! On their own, these roasted strawberries make the perfect snack or topping for vanilla ice cream. Here, they turn a regular muffin into the ultimate breakfast treat.

1. Preheat the oven to 350°F (180°C). Line a baking sheet with parchment paper and a muffin tin with 12 muffin liners.

2. To make the Roasted Strawberries, in a large mixing bowl toss the strawberries with the maple syrup and vanilla. Spread evenly on the prepared baking sheet and roast for 20 minutes, rotating the pan once, until syrupy. Let cool to room temperature on the baking sheet while you prepare the muffin batter.

3. In a large mixing bowl combine the yogurt, sugar, oil, maple syrup, vanilla and egg. Whisk until combined. Sift in the flour, baking soda, baking powder and salt. Add the oats. Stir until the batter just comes together. Gently fold in the Roasted Strawberries.

4. Divide the batter evenly among the muffin liners. Sprinkle the tops with a touch of sugar and oats. Bake for 20 to 25 minutes, until the tops bounce back when touched or until a toothpick inserted in the centre comes out clean. Turn out onto a rack and let cool for 15 minutes before serving. Store in an airtight container at room temperature for up to 2 days.

Rhubarb Oat Squares

These squares are like a hand-held fruit crisp that is loaded with buttery oat topping. I love the simplicity and versatility of this recipe. Changing the fruit in the filling means you can make these in any season, since the oat base works with just about any fruit filling you can think of. This rhubarb compote will always be my favourite; the combination of the natural sweet and sour flavours is like no other. I've added strawberries here as well—a common companion to rhubarb—to bring a touch of natural sweetness and create a beautiful deep pink hue. But the rhubarb remains the main attraction! These squares can be enjoyed as a quick breakfast or an afternoon snack or served for dessert.

1. Preheat the oven to 350°F (180°C). Line the bottom and sides of an 8-inch (20 cm) square baking pan with parchment paper.

2. To make the Rhubarb Filling, in a medium skillet combine the rhubarb, strawberries, sugar and lemon juice. Cook over medium heat, stirring occasionally, until the fruit has softened, about 10 minutes. Stir in the vanilla, nutmeg and salt. Transfer the mixture to a large mixing bowl. Using an immersion blender, purée the mixture until smooth (or mash with a fork). Let the filling cool slightly while you prepare the base.

3. To make the Oat Base, in a large mixing bowl whisk together the flour, oats, sugar, walnuts, cinnamon, nutmeg and salt. Pour in the butter and stir until the mixture comes together. Evenly spread half the oat mixture in the prepared pan and press down until a firm crust is formed. Evenly spread the Rhubarb Filling over the base. Sprinkle with the remaining oat mixture.

4. Bake for 30 minutes, or until the oats are golden brown and the rhubarb mixture is bubbling. Let cool completely before slicing and serving.

BAKER'S NOTE In the fall months I highly recommend switching out the rhubarb filling for a cup (250 mL) of apple butter. Or try a cup of blood orange curd in the winter. Get creative!

MAKES: *12 squares*

PREP TIME: *15 minutes*

COOK TIME: *40 minutes*

RHUBARB FILLING

1½ cups (375 mL) diced rhubarb

½ cup (125 mL) chopped strawberries

¼ cup (60 mL) turbinado sugar

1 tablespoon (15 mL) fresh lemon juice

1 teaspoon (5 mL) pure vanilla extract

Pinch of nutmeg

Pinch of fine salt

OAT BASE

2 cups (500 mL) all-purpose flour

2 cups (500 mL) old-fashioned rolled oats

1½ cups (375 mL) turbinado sugar

½ cup (125 mL) walnuts, roughly chopped

½ teaspoon (2 mL) cinnamon

¼ teaspoon (1 mL) nutmeg

¼ teaspoon (1 mL) fine salt

1 cup (250 mL) unsalted butter, melted

Rhubarb Upside-Down Cake

SERVES: *8*

PREP TIME: *15 minutes*

COOK TIME: *50 minutes*

CARAMEL RHUBARB

½ cup (125 mL) packed light brown sugar

⅓ cup (75 mL) unsalted butter

1 teaspoon (5 mL) pure vanilla extract

¼ teaspoon (1 mL) fine salt

6 to 8 stalks rhubarb, thinly sliced lengthwise

CAKE

¾ cup (175 mL) unsalted butter

1½ cups (375 mL) packed light brown sugar

3 large eggs

½ cup (125 mL) plain or vanilla full-fat yogurt

¼ cup (60 mL) water

1 tablespoon (15 mL) canola oil

2 teaspoons (10 mL) pure vanilla extract

2½ cups (625 mL) all-purpose flour

2 teaspoons (10 mL) baking powder

½ teaspoon (2 mL) salt

FOR SERVING

Fresh Whipped Cream (page 240) or vanilla ice cream

Remember that classic pineapple upside-down cake made with canned pineapple rings and maraschino cherries? Well, this cake is nothing like that. It features fresh rhubarb soaked in a simple brown sugar caramel sauce. The batter itself is not overly sweet, but the caramel sauce soaks into the cake and the rhubarb provides a hint of sourness, giving the finished cake a delicious balance of flavour.

1. Preheat the oven to 350°F (180°C).

2. To make the Caramel Rhubarb, in a large saucepan combine the brown sugar, butter, vanilla and salt. Stir over medium heat until the butter is melted and the sugar has fully dissolved. Add the sliced rhubarb and toss to coat. Remove from the heat and let cool to room temperature.

3. Pour the rhubarb mixture into an 8-inch (20 cm) round baking pan and arrange rhubarb in a vertical stripe pattern. Trim each slice to fit the pan. Set aside while you prepare the cake.

4. In the bowl of a stand mixer fitted with the paddle attachment, cream the butter with the brown sugar until light and fluffy, about 2 minutes. Add the eggs one at a time, beating after each addition. Add the yogurt, water, oil and vanilla and beat until well incorporated. Sift in the flour, baking powder and salt. Beat until the batter is lump-free, about 60 seconds. Pour the batter over the Caramel Rhubarb and smooth the top.

5. Bake for 45 to 50 minutes, until the top bounces back when touched or until a toothpick inserted in the centre comes out clean. Transfer to a rack and let cool for 1 to 2 hours before flipping onto a plate and removing the pan. Serve with Fresh Whipped Cream or vanilla ice cream.

Maple Carrot Cake

My neighbour used to make the best carrot cake, and I spent years trying to create one as good as hers. Once I worked out a recipe that was a close imitation, it became my best-kept secret—I guess the Italian in me likes to keep tried-and-true recipes close to my heart. Now I've decided this recipe needs to be shared! I love using young spring carrots here, making this cake my go-to every Easter. Some people prefer their carrot cake kept simple, but I like mine loaded with carrots, pineapple, coconut and walnuts. If you like raisins, go ahead and fold in a cup of golden raisins too.

1. Preheat the oven to 325°F (160°C). Grease three 8-inch (20 cm) round cake pans.

2. To make the Carrot Cake, in a large mixing bowl sift together the flour, baking soda, salt, cinnamon, ginger and nutmeg.

3. In a separate large mixing bowl beat together the eggs, sugar, oil, butter, maple syrup, and vanilla until fluffy, about 2 minutes. Stir in the carrots, pineapple, coconut and walnuts. Gradually add the flour mixture, beating until just combined.

4. Evenly divide the batter among the prepared cake pans. Bake for 25 to 30 minutes, until the top bounces back when touched or until a toothpick inserted in the centre comes out clean. Transfer to a rack and let the cakes cool completely.

5. To make the Maple Cream Cheese Frosting, in the bowl of a stand mixer fitted with the paddle attachment, beat the butter, sugar, maple syrup and vanilla on medium speed until fluffy, about 10 minutes. Scrape down the sides of the bowl, then beat in the cream cheese 1 ounce (30 g) at a time until just incorporated.

6. Remove the cooled cakes from their pans. Using a long serrated knife, level the top of each cake, if necessary.

Continues

SERVES: *10 to 12*

PREP TIME: *60 minutes*

COOK TIME: *25 minutes*

CARROT CAKE

3 cups (750 mL) all-purpose flour

1 tablespoon (15 mL) baking soda

1 teaspoon (5 mL) fine salt

2 teaspoons (10 mL) cinnamon

½ teaspoon (2 mL) ground ginger

½ teaspoon (2 mL) nutmeg

4 large eggs

2 cups (500 mL) turbinado sugar

¾ cup (175 mL) vegetable oil

½ cup (125 mL) unsalted butter, melted

⅓ cup (75 mL) pure maple syrup

1 tablespoon (15 mL) pure vanilla extract

2 cups (500 mL) finely grated carrots

1 cup (250 mL) canned crushed pineapple, drained

1 cup (250 mL) unsweetened shredded coconut

1 cup (250 mL) walnuts or pecans, roughly chopped

MAPLE CREAM CHEESE FROSTING

1 cup (250 mL) unsalted butter, room temperature

4 cups (1 L) icing sugar

¼ cup (60 mL) pure maple syrup

1 teaspoon (5 mL) pure vanilla extract

16 ounces (450 g) full-fat cream cheese, cold

½ cup (125 mL) finely chopped walnuts or pecans

7. Place one cake layer on a cake stand or cake turntable and dollop approximately ¾ cup (175 mL) frosting onto the middle. Using an offset spatula, smooth the frosting flat, spreading it to the edges. Place a second cake layer on top and gently press down to stabilize it. Spread another ¾ cup (175 mL) frosting over the top and smooth flat. Top with the final layer of cake top down and gently press down to stabilize and level it. Dollop 2 cups (500 mL) frosting onto the top and use the offset spatula to gently work the frosting evenly over the top and down the sides. Be sure to coat every inch of the cake with frosting.

8. For a smooth finish, hold the edge of the offset spatula or a bench scraper against the cake and slowly turn the cake. This will remove excess frosting and leave a clean edge. For a rustic finish, use an offset spatula or the back of a spoon in a swooping motion to create swirls.

9. If desired, transfer the remaining frosting to a piping bag fitted with a medium star tip and pipe dollops over the top. Lastly, press the walnuts around the bottom edge, creating a border 1 inch (2.5 cm) high.

10. Serve the cake immediately or store in the fridge, uncovered, for up to 24 hours.

Strawberry Rhubarb Pie

Strawberry rhubarb pie is a classic. Although I ate these pies throughout my childhood—my mom would make them all spring and summer long—I never had a real sense of what rhubarb was, what it looked like or that it was actually a vegetable. Funny, considering how it became one of my favourites to bake with in spring. And I know I can't go long without it, so I always freeze a bag of it for baking in the winter months. You never know when a craving will strike!

SERVES: *8*

PREP TIME: *20 minutes*

COOK TIME: *60 minutes*

4 cups (1 L) quartered strawberries

3 cups (750 mL) sliced rhubarb

1 cup (250 mL) turbinado sugar, plus more for sprinkling

⅓ cup (75 mL) cornstarch

1 tablespoon (15 mL) fresh lemon juice

1½ teaspoons (7 mL) pure vanilla extract

1 batch Double Pie Dough (page 243), chilled

1 large egg

1 teaspoon (5 mL) water

1. In a large mixing bowl combine the strawberries, rhubarb, sugar, cornstarch, lemon juice and vanilla. Toss to coat. Set aside while you roll out the dough.

2. On a lightly floured surface, roll out half the pie dough until ⅛ inch (3 mm) thick. Gently lift and transfer the dough to a 9-inch (23 cm) pie plate and press the dough into the bottom and sides of the plate. Trim the edges, leaving a ½-inch (1 cm) overhang. Pour in the strawberry rhubarb filling.

3. To make the lattice top, roll out the remaining pie dough until ¼ inch (5 mm) thick. Using a pastry cutter, cut the dough into strips ½ inch (1 cm) wide. Evenly lay 5 strips vertically over the filling. Fold back every other strip halfway. Place another strip horizontally across the filling, right next to the folds, and unfold the folded strips over it. Fold back the opposite vertical strips and place a second strip of dough horizontally across the filling, about ½ inch (1 cm) from the first horizontal strip. Unfold the folded strips over the horizontal strip. Repeat on both halves of the pie until the weave is complete. Trim the ends of the strips, leaving a ½-inch (1 cm) overhang. Fold under the overhangs, then crimp the edges. To crimp the edges, place an index finger on the lip of the pie plate and pinch around that finger with the index finger and thumb of your other hand, holding the dough in between.

Continues

4. In a small bowl beat the egg with the water. Brush the egg wash over the dough and sprinkle with a touch of sugar, if desired.

5. Place the pie in the fridge to chill and preheat the oven to 450°F (230°C).

6. Bake the pie for 10 minutes, then turn down the temperature to 350°F (180°C) and bake for an additional 50 to 60 minutes. If the top browns too quickly, tent with foil. Once the fruit begins to bubble and the pastry is golden brown, the pie is ready. Transfer to a rack and let the pie cool completely before serving.

Toasted Coconut Cream Pie

I love coconut cream pie, and I love making it for Easter. Every holiday deserves a pie, and Easter is no exception! When I was growing up, my neighbour across the street would bake my sisters and me two things: carrot cake and coconut cream pie. She was an amazing baker and we would fight over the last slice every single time. I always won—nothing gets between me and my love for pie. I prefer a graham cracker crust here instead of a traditional pie crust, as it is easier to make and has much more flavour.

1. Preheat the oven to 375°F (190°C).

2. To make the Graham Cracker Pie Crust, in a medium mixing bowl stir together the graham cracker crumbs, sugar, butter, vanilla and salt until well mixed. Transfer the mixture to a 9-inch (23 cm) pie plate and press over the bottom and up the sides into a firm, even crust. Bake for 10 minutes. Transfer to a rack and let cool.

3. To make the Coconut Cream Filling, in a medium saucepan combine the egg yolks, coconut milk, whole milk, cream, sugar, cornstarch and salt. Whisk until well combined. Bring to a boil, stirring constantly, over medium heat. Once the mixture begins to bubble and thicken, cook for an additional minute. Remove from the heat and stir in the butter and vanilla until the butter is melted. Stir in the toasted coconut. Scrape the filling into the cooled graham cracker crust and chill for 4 to 6 hours.

4. Before serving, prepare the Fresh Whipped Cream. Using an offset spatula, top the chilled pie with the whipped cream. Sprinkle with additional coconut, if desired.

SERVES: *6 to 8*

PREP TIME: *4 hours*

COOK TIME: *25 minutes*

GRAHAM CRACKER PIE CRUST

2 cups (500 mL) graham cracker crumbs

¼ cup (60 mL) granulated sugar

½ cup (125 mL) unsalted butter, melted

1 teaspoon (5 mL) pure vanilla extract

Pinch of fine salt

COCONUT CREAM FILLING

4 large egg yolks

1½ cups (375 mL) full-fat canned coconut milk

½ cup (125 mL) whole milk

½ cup (125 mL) heavy cream

1 cup (250 mL) turbinado sugar

¼ cup (60 mL) cornstarch

½ teaspoon (2 mL) fine salt

1 tablespoon (15 mL) unsalted butter

2 teaspoons (10 mL) pure vanilla extract

2 cups (500 mL) toasted unsweetened shredded coconut, plus more for topping

1 batch Fresh Whipped Cream (page 240)

Lemon Thyme Tart

SERVES: *6 to 8*

PREP TIME: *15 minutes*

COOK TIME: *50 minutes*

LEMON THYME SHORTBREAD CRUST

1 cup (250 mL) unsalted butter, room temperature

½ cup (125 mL) turbinado sugar

1 teaspoon (5 mL) pure vanilla extract

2¼ cups (550 mL) all-purpose flour

Pinch of fine salt

1 teaspoon (5 mL) roughly chopped fresh thyme

1 teaspoon (5 mL) grated lemon zest

LEMON FILLING

6 large eggs

2½ cups (625 mL) granulated sugar

1 cup (250 mL) all-purpose flour

2 teaspoons (10 mL) grated lemon zest

1 cup (250 mL) fresh lemon juice

1 teaspoon (5 mL) roughly chopped fresh thyme

1 teaspoon (5 mL) pure vanilla extract

Icing sugar, for dusting

This light, tangy tart is the perfect dessert to make in early spring with the last of winter's citrus. As a kid, lemon meringue pie was one of my favourite desserts to make with my mom—although, truth be told, I would flick aside the meringue and just eat the lemon filling. It got to the point where my mom would just give me a separate bowl of lemon curd to eat so I wouldn't mangle the pie. Nowadays, I make this meringue-free tart with a shortbread crust, combining my favourite cookie and lemon filling into one dessert. I love including savoury herbs in sweet desserts, and here the thyme offers a hit of freshness, but it is subtle and doesn't overpower the flavours.

1. Preheat the oven to 350°F (180°C).

2. To make the Shortbread Crust, in a large mixing bowl cream together the butter and sugar until fluffy, about 2 minutes. Add the vanilla and mix until incorporated. Sift in the flour and salt, then add the thyme and lemon zest. Beat just until the dough comes together.

3. Turn the dough out onto a floured surface and shape into a disc. Roll out to an 11-inch (28 cm) circle and transfer to a 9-inch (23 cm) tart pan with a removable bottom. Evenly press the dough into the bottom and sides of the pan and trim the edges. Chill for 30 minutes while the oven heats.

4. Bake the crust for 15 minutes while you prepare the filling. (The crust will be partially cooked by that time and will continue baking after the filling is added.)

5. To make the Lemon Filling, in a large mixing bowl whisk together the eggs, sugar, flour, lemon zest, lemon juice, thyme and vanilla. As soon as the crust has baked for 15 minutes, pour in the filling and bake for an additional 35 to 40 minutes, or until the filling is firm but the centre slightly jiggles.

6. Transfer to a rack and let the tart cool to room temperature for at least 2 hours before serving. The filling will set as the tart cools. Remove pan sides, slice, dust with icing sugar and serve.

Mango Coconut Crisp

In my neck of the woods it is not often you come across mangoes in baked goods, but I couldn't resist incorporating the mango's sweet, buttery texture into a tropical coconut crisp. It is in our early spring that tropical mangoes are in season and begin to pop up in grocery stores everywhere. This dish is best made with these ripe, in-season fruits. I know it's tempting to use frozen mangoes, but they lack the fresh flavour and texture needed for this crisp.

1. Preheat the oven to 350°F (180°C).

2. To make the Mango Filling, in a large mixing bowl toss together the mango, sugar, cornstarch, salt, lemon juice and vanilla. Pour the filling into a 9- x 12-inch (3 L) baking dish and set aside while you prepare the topping.

3. To make the Coconut Crisp Topping, in a large mixing bowl combine the oats, flour, coconut, sugar, cinnamon and salt. Add the cubed butter. Using your hands, work the butter into the oat mixture until a crumb-like mixture is formed. Evenly sprinkle the topping over the mango filling.

4. Bake for 45 to 50 minutes, until the topping is golden brown and the fruit filling is bubbling. Serve warm or room temperature topped with Fresh Whipped Cream.

SERVES: *6 to 8*

PREP TIME: *20 minutes*

COOK TIME: *45 minutes*

MANGO FILLING

6 cups (1.5 L) peeled and diced fresh mango

½ cup (125 mL) turbinado sugar

2 tablespoons (30 mL) cornstarch

½ teaspoon (2 mL) fine salt

1 tablespoon (15 mL) fresh lemon juice

1 teaspoon (5 mL) pure vanilla extract

COCONUT CRISP TOPPING

1 cup (250 mL) old-fashioned rolled oats

1 cup (250 mL) all-purpose flour

1 cup (250 mL) unsweetened flaked coconut

½ cup (125 mL) turbinado sugar

½ teaspoon (2 mL) cinnamon

½ teaspoon (2 mL) fine salt

⅔ cup (150 mL) unsalted butter, cold and cubed

FOR SERVING

Fresh Whipped Cream (page 240)

Cherry Rhubarb Cobbler

SERVES: *6 to 8*

PREP TIME: *20 minutes*

COOK TIME: *50 minutes*

COBBLER TOPPING

2 cups (500 mL) all-purpose flour

1 cup (250 mL) turbinado sugar

2 teaspoons (10 mL) baking
   powder

½ teaspoon (2 mL) fine salt

¼ teaspoon (1 mL) nutmeg

¾ cup (175 mL) unsalted butter,
   cold and cubed

½ cup (125 mL) whole milk

1 teaspoon (5 mL) pure vanilla
   extract

CHERRY RHUBARB FILLING

4 cups (1 L) pitted and halved
   sweet cherries

3 cups (750 mL) thinly sliced
   rhubarb

1 cup (250 mL) turbinado sugar

3 tablespoons (45 mL) cornstarch

Pinch of nutmeg

1 tablespoon (15 mL) fresh
   lemon juice

1 teaspoon (5 mL) pure vanilla
   extract

FOR SERVING

Vanilla ice cream or Fresh
   Whipped Cream (page 240)

Rhubarb doesn't *always* have to be paired with strawberries. This cherry rhubarb cobbler is a perfect dessert to make in the late spring and early summer, around the time local cherries start popping up at farmers' markets and the rhubarb plants are looking wild in the garden. I prefer a cobbler with a healthy amount of topping (similar to my crisps and crumbles), and this recipe offers just that. If you are a fan of the classic strawberry rhubarb combination, switching out the cherries for strawberries works too.

1. Preheat the oven to 350°F (180°C).

2. To make the Cobbler Topping, in a large mixing bowl stir together the flour, sugar, baking powder, salt and nutmeg. Add the butter. Using your hands, work in the butter until the mixture forms pea-sized crumbles. Add the milk and vanilla and continue to mix until the mixture begins to clump together slightly. Set aside while you prepare the filling.

3. To make the Cherry Rhubarb Filling, in a separate large mixing bowl combine the cherries, rhubarb, sugar, cornstarch, nutmeg, lemon juice and vanilla. Toss to coat. Pour the filling into a 9- x 12-inch (3 L) baking dish. Top with the Cobbler Topping.

4. Bake for 50 minutes, or until the topping is golden brown and the fruit filling is bubbling. Serve warm with vanilla ice cream or whipped cream.

Cherry Almond Dutch Baby

Not everyone is familiar with the Dutch baby, which I would classify as a breakfast pastry. The best way to describe it is as a cross between a pancake and a Yorkshire pudding. It is slightly sweet and often topped with fresh fruit and maple syrup like a pancake, but has the egg taste and puff factor of a Yorkshire pudding. This dish whips up quickly too. Throw the ingredients into a blender, pour the batter into a piping hot pan and watch it rise before your eyes. I love the combination of cherry and almond here, but don't be shy! Make this dish throughout the seasons and top it with whatever you have on hand. I prefer it in the late spring, before the dog days of summer roll around and heating my oven is a lot less appealing.

1. Place an 8-inch (20 cm) cast-iron skillet in the oven and preheat the oven to 425°F (220°C).

2. In a blender, pulse the eggs until frothy. Add the flour, milk, vanilla, almond extract and salt. Blend until smooth. Let the mixture rest for at least 15 minutes while the oven heats.

3. Once the oven is heated, remove the skillet and add the butter. Carefully swirl the melting butter to coat the pan's edges. Be careful, as the pan will be smoking hot!

4. Immediately pour the batter into the buttered pan. Quickly sprinkle with 1 cup (250 mL) of the cherries and the sliced almonds. Bake for 20 minutes, until the dough puffs. Do not open the oven during this time or the Dutch baby will not properly rise.

5. Top with the remaining cherries, dust with icing sugar and drizzle with maple syrup. Serve immediately.

SERVES: *2 to 4*

PREP TIME: *30 minutes*

COOK TIME: *20 minutes*

3 large eggs, room temperature

⅔ cup (150 mL) all-purpose flour

⅔ cup (150 mL) whole milk, room temperature

1 teaspoon (5 mL) pure vanilla extract

1 teaspoon (5 mL) pure almond extract

⅛ teaspoon (0.5 mL) fine salt

4 tablespoons (60 mL) unsalted butter, room temperature

2 cups (500 mL) pitted and halved sweet cherries, divided

1 tablespoon (15 mL) sliced almonds

1 tablespoon (15 mL) icing sugar, for dusting

Maple syrup, for serving

Asparagus, Prosciutto and Wild Mushroom Frittata

SERVES: *4 to 6*

PREP TIME: *15 minutes*

COOK TIME: *40 minutes*

2 tablespoons (30 mL) unsalted butter

2 tablespoons (30 mL) extra-virgin olive oil

2 cloves garlic, minced

1 medium onion, finely chopped

2 cups (500 mL) sliced wild mushrooms (such as cremini, shiitake and chanterelle)

Salt and pepper

¼ pound (115 g) asparagus, trimmed and roughly chopped

6 large eggs

1 cup (250 mL) panko breadcrumbs

1 cup (250 mL) freshly grated Romano or Parmesan cheese

4 ounces (115 g) thinly sliced prosciutto, roughly chopped

The frittata is my all-time favourite egg-based breakfast and brunch dish. It is the dish that made me fall in love with eggs; before that, I would only eat scrambled eggs covered with ketchup (with a ketchup-to-eggs ratio of 2:1). However, frittatas feature so many other flavours that the eggs become more subtle. The flavours in this particular frittata combine my favourite things into one dish. I think of this as a low-maintenance quiche that I would happily serve at any morning gathering. The leftovers (if you are lucky to have any) work great between two toasted slices of bread.

1. Preheat the oven to 350°F (180°C). Bring a large pot of water to a boil.

2. In a 9-inch (23 cm) cast-iron skillet over medium heat melt the butter, then add the olive oil and garlic. Cook, stirring, until the garlic is fragrant, about 30 seconds. Add the onion and mushrooms, and season with salt and pepper. Cook until the onions begin to turn translucent and the mushrooms have softened, about 5 minutes.

3. While the filling is cooking, add the asparagus to the pot of boiling water and cook for 2 minutes. Remove the asparagus and immediately rinse under cold water. Add the blanched asparagus to the skillet and cook for an additional minute. Remove from the heat and let cool slightly.

4. In a large mixing bowl whisk the eggs until frothy. Whisk in the panko, cheese and prosciutto. Fold the mushroom mixture into the egg mixture, then season with salt and pepper. Pour the filling back into the skillet.

5. Bake for 30 minutes, or until the top is golden brown and the filling is firm. Serve immediately.

Artichoke, Sausage and Wild Mushroom Quiche

This quiche packs so much flavour, you will want to eat it for breakfast, lunch and dinner. With spring artichokes, mushrooms and sausage, it's incredibly hearty and filling. Maybe it's the Italian in me, but I love incorporating sausage into just about anything. It is versatile and brings a ton of flavour to any dish. This quiche would be perfect served for Easter or Mother's Day brunch.

1. On a lightly floured surface, roll out the pie dough until ⅛ inch (3 mm) thick. Gently lift and transfer the dough to a 9-inch (23 cm) pie plate and press the dough into the bottom and sides of the plate. Trim the edges, leaving a 1-inch (2.5 cm) overhang. Fold under the overhang and crimp the edges. Use your index fingers to push the dough between your thumb. Refrigerate while you prepare the filling.

2. To a large skillet over medium heat, add the olive oil and sausage. Break up the sausage and cook until golden brown. Remove the sausage from the pan and set aside in a bowl.

3. Add the butter, shallots, garlic and mushrooms to the skillet. Cook, stirring frequently, until the mushrooms have softened, about 10 minutes.

4. Add the artichoke hearts, ¼ cup (60 mL) of the parsley and the reserved browned sausage. Season with salt and pepper. Cook for an additional 2 minutes, stirring. Remove from the heat and let cool to room temperature.

5. While the filling cools, preheat the oven to 375°F (190°C).

6. In a large mixing bowl whisk together the eggs, cream, milk and remaining ¼ cup (60 mL) parsley. Stir in the cooled artichoke mixture and the Asiago. Season with salt and pepper.

7. Pour the filling into the chilled pie shell and bake for 40 to 50 minutes, until the top is golden brown and the filling has set. It should be firm and not jiggle.

SERVES: *6 to 8*

PREP TIME: *25 minutes*

COOK TIME: *65 minutes*

1 batch Single Pie Dough (page 243), chilled

2 tablespoons (30 mL) extra-virgin olive oil

1 pound (450 g) Italian sausage, casings removed

2 tablespoons (30 mL) unsalted butter

4 shallots, minced

2 cloves garlic, minced

3 cups (750 mL) sliced wild mushrooms (such as cremini, shiitake and chanterelle)

1 cup (250 mL) artichoke hearts (cooked fresh, canned or jarred), roughly chopped

½ cup (125 mL) chopped fresh parsley, divided

Salt and pepper

4 large eggs

1 cup (250 mL) heavy cream

1 cup (250 mL) whole milk

1½ cups (375 mL) grated Asiago cheese

Spinach and Feta Quiche

After recipe testing countless spanakopita recipes to create my Spanakopita Triangles (page 58), I knew the flavours in those pastries would taste delicious in a quiche. I was right! This quiche shakes up the classic spanakopita in a savoury, rich brunch treat. Don't expect any leftovers!

SERVES: *6 to 8*

PREP TIME: *20 minutes*

COOK TIME: *50 minutes*

1 pound (450 g) fresh spinach, roughly chopped

1 batch Single Pie Dough (page 243), chilled

2 tablespoons (30 mL) unsalted butter

2 tablespoons (30 mL) extra-virgin olive oil

2 cloves garlic, minced

4 shallots, minced

Salt and pepper

5 large eggs

1 cup (250 mL) heavy cream

1 cup (250 mL) whole milk

½ cup (125 mL) roughly chopped fresh parsley

1 cup (250 mL) crumbled goat's milk feta cheese

1. Preheat the oven to 375°F (190°C).

2. Bring a large pot of water to a boil. Add the spinach and cook until wilted, about 2 minutes. Drain the spinach, rinse with cold water and squeeze out as much water as possible. This should yield approximately 1 packed cup (250 mL) of spinach. Set aside.

3. On a lightly floured surface, roll out the pie dough until ⅛ inch (3 mm) thick. Gently lift and transfer the dough to a 9-inch (23 cm) pie plate and press the dough into the bottom and sides of the plate. Trim the dough edges, leaving a 1-inch (2.5 cm) overhang of dough. Fold under the overhang and crimp the edges. To crimp the edges, place an index finger on the lip of the pie plate and pinch around that finger with the index finger and thumb of your other hand, holding the dough in between. Refrigerate while you prepare the filling.

4. To a large skillet over medium heat, add the butter, olive oil, garlic and shallots. Cook, stirring frequently, until the shallots have softened and are translucent, about 5 minutes. Add the squeezed spinach and cook for an additional 2 minutes, stirring to break up the spinach. Season with salt and pepper. Remove from the heat and let cool for 15 minutes.

5. In a large mixing bowl whisk together the eggs, cream, milk and parsley. Stir in the cooled spinach mixture and feta. Season with salt and pepper.

6. Pour the filling into the prepared pie shell. Bake for 40 to 50 minutes, until the top is golden brown and the filling has set. It should be firm and not jiggle. Let stand for 5 minutes before serving.

Leek and Pancetta Tart

SERVES: *6*

PREP TIME: *20 minutes*

COOK TIME: *45 minutes*

CHEDDAR TART DOUGH

1¼ cups (300 mL) all-purpose
flour

½ teaspoon (2 mL) fine salt

½ teaspoon (2 mL) pepper

½ cup (125 mL) unsalted butter,
cold and cubed

½ cup (125 mL) grated aged
cheddar cheese

3 tablespoons (45 mL) ice water

1 large egg yolk

LEEK PANCETTA FILLING

1 tablespoon (15 mL) unsalted
butter

1 tablespoon (15 mL) extra-virgin
olive oil

1 clove garlic, minced

2 leeks, dark green tops removed,
thinly sliced

4 ounces (115 g) thinly sliced
pancetta, roughly chopped

Salt and pepper

4 large eggs

1 cup (250 mL) grated aged
cheddar cheese

¾ cup (175 mL) heavy cream

Leeks are vibrant in the springtime, and in this dish they are beautifully complemented by salty pancetta. This tart would be perfect for an Easter brunch. I pack a little extra flavour into the tart dough, too, by incorporating cheddar cheese. This is one of my favourite tricks—who doesn't love extra cheese!

1. To make the Cheddar Tart Dough, in a large mixing bowl whisk together the flour, salt and pepper. Add the butter. Using a pastry cutter or your hands, work in the butter until the mixture forms pea-sized crumbs. Fold in the cheddar cheese.

2. In a small bowl whisk together the water and egg yolk. Pour the egg mixture over the flour mixture and use your hands to work the mixture together until a dough begins to form. Turn the dough out onto a floured surface and shape it into a disc. Wrap in plastic wrap and refrigerate for 2 hours.

3. On a lightly floured surface, roll out the dough to ¼-inch (5 mm) thickness. Gently lift and transfer the dough to a 9-inch (23 cm) tart pan with a removable bottom. Evenly press the dough into the bottom and sides of the pan. Trim the edges. Place back in the refrigerator while you prepare the filling.

4. To make the Leek Pancetta Filling, in a large saucepan over medium heat melt together the butter and olive oil. Add the garlic and leeks and cook, stirring occasionally, until the leeks begin to turn translucent, about 5 minutes. Stir in the pancetta and season with salt and pepper. Cook for an additional 2 minutes, until the pancetta is crispy and brown. Remove from the heat and let cool to room temperature.

5. While the filling cools, preheat the oven to 350°F (180°C).

6. In a large mixing bowl whisk together the eggs, cheese and cream. Fold in the cooled leek mixture. Season with salt and pepper. Pour the filling into the chilled tart shell.

7. Bake for 30 minutes, or until the top is golden and the filling has slightly puffed. Let stand for 5 minutes before slicing. Serve warm.

Asparagus Balsamic Tart

Every year I get excited when spring arrives and asparagus is (finally!) in season. Throughout April and May, I just can't get enough. I love the simple preparation of roasting it with olive oil, salt and pepper or, when I'm feeling a little extra fancy, wrapping it in prosciutto. This tart is for the asparagus lover in all of us.

1. Preheat the oven to 375°F (190°C).

2. To make the Balsamic Caramelized Onions, in a large saucepan over low heat, combine the onions, garlic, butter and oil. Cook slowly, stirring every minute or two, until the onions are translucent and soft, about 20 minutes. Add the balsamic vinegar and mustard, and season with salt and pepper. Stir until well incorporated. Increase the heat to medium and cook for an additional 5 minutes, until the onions are caramelized. Set aside until ready to use.

3. To make the Asparagus Balsamic Tart, bring a large pot of water to a boil. Meanwhile, on a sheet of parchment paper, roll out the puff pastry to an 8- x 12-inch (20 x 30 cm) rectangle. The pastry should be ¼ inch (5 mm) thick. Transfer the pastry on parchment paper to a baking sheet and trim the edges straight, if desired. Evenly spread the Balsamic Caramelized Onions over the pastry leaving a ½ inch (1 cm) border, then evenly sprinkle with the Gruyère. Bake for 10 minutes, or until the cheese begins to melt.

4. While the tart is baking, add the asparagus to the boiling water and cook for 2 minutes. Remove the asparagus and immediately rinse under cold water. Pat the asparagus dry with paper towel. In a medium mixing bowl toss the blanched asparagus with the oil and salt and pepper to taste.

5. Top the partially baked tart with a row of asparagus and bake for an additional 7 to 10 minutes, until the asparagus begins to brown. Serve immediately.

SERVES: *2 to 4*

PREP TIME: *15 minutes*

COOK TIME: *50 minutes*

BALSAMIC CARAMELIZED ONIONS

3 medium onions, thinly sliced

2 cloves garlic, minced

4 tablespoons (60 mL) unsalted butter

2 tablespoons (30 mL) extra-virgin olive oil

1 tablespoon (15 mL) balsamic vinegar

1 teaspoon (5 mL) Dijon mustard

Salt and pepper

ASPARAGUS BALSAMIC TART

1 sheet (8 ounces/225 g) frozen all-butter puff pastry, thawed

2 cups (500 mL) grated Gruyère cheese

½ pound (225 g) asparagus, trimmed

1 tablespoon (15 mL) extra-virgin olive oil

Salt and pepper

Rainbow Carrot Tart

SERVES: *4 to 6*

PREP TIME: *15 minutes*

COOK TIME: *45 minutes*

ROASTED RAINBOW CARROTS

5 or 6 rainbow carrots, peeled and quartered lengthwise

2 tablespoons (30 mL) extra-virgin olive oil

1 tablespoon (15 mL) raw honey

1½ teaspoons (7 mL) balsamic vinegar

1 teaspoon (5 mL) chopped fresh thyme

Salt and pepper

RAINBOW CARROT TART

1 sheet (8 ounces/225 g) frozen all-butter puff pastry, thawed

½ cup (125 mL) soft goat cheese

1 tablespoon (15 mL) raw honey

1 teaspoon (5 mL) chopped fresh thyme

Salt and pepper

I cannot get over the vibrant colours of rainbow carrots—nature at its best! I first made the roasted carrots in this recipe as an amazing side dish, but here I take things one step further and work them into a stunning tart. With its distinctive flavours of goat cheese and local honey, this tart makes for a show-stopping appetizer. Nothing beats the colours of rainbow carrots found at farmers' markets in the spring, but you can also make this year round with regular carrots.

1. Preheat the oven to 375°F (190°C). Line 2 baking sheets with parchment paper.

2. To make the Roasted Rainbow Carrots, in a large mixing bowl toss together the carrots, oil, honey, balsamic vinegar, thyme, and salt and pepper to taste. Spread evenly on one of the prepared baking sheets and roast for 20 to 25 minutes, until the carrots have softened. Remove from the oven, but keep the oven set to 375°F (190°C).

3. For the Rainbow Carrot Tart, on a lightly floured surface roll out the puff pastry to an 8- x 10-inch (20 x 25 cm) rectangle. Using a fork, poke a line about ½ inch (1 cm) inside the edge of the pastry to create a border. Transfer to the remaining prepared baking sheet. Bake for 10 minutes.

4. While the pastry bakes, stir together the goat cheese, honey, thyme, and salt and pepper to taste.

5. Remove the puff pastry from the oven and gently spread with the goat cheese mixture, staying inside the border. Evenly top with the roasted carrots. Place back in the oven and bake for an additional 10 minutes, or until the puff pastry is fully cooked and golden brown. Serve immediately.

Greens and Wild Mushroom Pot Pies

This is not your average chicken pot pie. Lighter than your typical pot pie, my twist on the classic winter comfort dish is filled to the brim with fresh spring greens. It can easily be transformed into a vegetarian dish, simply by replacing the roasted chicken with an equal amount of wild mushrooms. I keep this extra simple by topping it with rounds of puff pastry.

1. Preheat the oven to 400°F (200°C).

2. In a large saucepan over medium heat, melt the butter with the garlic. Once the butter has melted, add the onion, carrots, mushrooms and thyme. Cook, stirring occasionally, until the carrots have softened and the onions are translucent, about 5 minutes. Add the green and red Swiss chards and cook, stirring occasionally, for an additional 2 minutes.

3. In a large liquid measuring cup whisk together the flour, chicken stock and cream. Pour into the pan, constantly stirring, and simmer until thickened. The mixture should coat the back of a spoon. Remove from the heat and stir in the shredded chicken and Gruyère.

4. Divide the mixture among four 1-cup (250 mL) mini cocottes or ramekins.

5. On a lightly floured surface, roll out the puff pastry. Cut out 4 circles about ½ inch (1 cm) wider than the cocotte or ramekin top. Cover each cocotte with a round of puff pastry and pinch down the edges. Brush each with the egg wash.

6. Place the ramekins on a baking sheet and bake for 20 minutes, or until the pastry is puffed and golden brown. Let stand for 5 minutes before serving.

SERVES: *4*

PREP TIME: *15 minutes*

COOK TIME: *35 minutes*

4 tablespoons (60 mL) unsalted butter

2 cloves garlic, minced

1 large onion, thinly sliced

2 medium carrots, peeled and diced

3 cups (750 mL) sliced wild mushrooms (such as cremini, shiitake and chanterelle)

2 teaspoons (10 mL) chopped fresh thyme

6 ounces (170 g) green Swiss chard, stemmed and chopped

6 ounces (170 g) red Swiss chard, stemmed and chopped

3 tablespoons (45 mL) all-purpose flour

1½ cups (375 mL) low-sodium chicken stock

½ cup (125 mL) heavy cream

1 roasted chicken breast, shredded

1 cup (250 mL) grated Gruyère cheese

1 sheet (8 ounces/225 g) frozen all-butter puff pastry, thawed

1 egg, whisked, for egg wash

Leek, Wild Mushroom and Bacon Strata

4 tablespoons (60 mL) unsalted butter

2 tablespoons (30 mL) extra-virgin olive oil

2 cloves garlic, minced

3 cups (750 mL) sliced wild mushrooms (such as shiitake, chanterelle and oyster)

2 leeks, dark green ends removed, thinly sliced

Salt and pepper

6 large eggs

1½ cups (375 mL) whole milk

10 strips bacon, cooked and roughly chopped

1½ cups (375 mL) grated smoked Gouda cheese

8 cups (2 L) cubed whole-grain bread

A strata is a breakfast casserole often made with bread, eggs and cheese. I love how simple this one-dish breakfast bake is to prepare. I recommend putting it together the night before; it can be easily tucked away in your refrigerator, ready to be baked and served hot in the morning. This strata is packed with loads of seasonal flavours. Plus, I don't think you can ever go wrong with bacon. I use a whole-grain bread in this bake to provide a hearty and wholesome flavour, but a fresh loaf of white bread works just as well.

1. Preheat the oven to 375°F (190°C). Grease a 9- x 12-inch (3 L) baking dish.

2. In a large skillet over medium heat melt the butter. Add the oil and garlic and cook, stirring, for 30 seconds. Add the mushrooms and leeks, then season with salt and pepper. Cook, stirring frequently, until the mushrooms have softened and the leeks begin to turn translucent. Remove from the heat and let cool slightly.

3. In a large mixing bowl whisk together the eggs and milk. Fold in the cooked bacon, Gouda and leek mixture. Add the bread cubes and toss until the bread is well coated. Pour into the prepared baking dish.

4. Bake for 45 to 50 minutes, until the top is golden brown and the egg custard has set. The centre should be firm and not jiggly. Let stand for 5 minutes before serving.

Spinach and Chard Gratin

SERVES: *4 to 6*

PREP TIME: *15 minutes*

COOK TIME: *40 minutes*

2 pounds (900 g) fresh spinach, roughly chopped

1 pound (450 g) red Swiss chard, stemmed and roughly chopped

2 tablespoons (30 mL) unsalted butter

2 tablespoons (30 mL) extra-virgin olive oil

1½ cups (375 mL) chopped white onion

2 large cloves garlic, minced

Salt and pepper

2 tablespoons (30 mL) all-purpose flour

¾ cup (175 mL) heavy cream

1½ cups (375 mL) grated Fontina cheese, divided

½ cup (125 mL) panko breadcrumbs

This might possibly be one of the most delicious ways to eat your spring greens! Creamy and filled with melty Fontina cheese, this gratin will have everyone asking for seconds or thirds. This recipe works beautifully with any greens, but the combination of spinach and Swiss chard is my favourite. This would be perfect served alongside roast chicken.

1. Preheat the oven to 400°F (200°C).

2. Bring a large pot of water to a boil. Add the spinach and Swiss chard and cook until wilted, about 2 minutes. Drain, rinse with cold water and squeeze out any excess water. This should yield approximately 3 packed cups (750 mL) of greens. Set aside.

3. In a large saucepan over medium heat, melt the butter with the olive oil. Add the onion and garlic and cook, stirring frequently, until the onion begins to turn translucent, about 5 minutes. Season with salt and pepper.

4. Stir in the cooked spinach and Swiss chard. Sprinkle with the flour and cook for an additional minute or two while constantly stirring.

5. Pour in the cream, then add ¾ cup (175 mL) of the Fontina. Stir until the mixture thickens slightly and the cheese is fully melted.

6. Spread the mixture evenly in a medium casserole dish. Sprinkle with the remaining ¾ cup (175 mL) Fontina and the panko.

7. Bake for 25 minutes, or until the top is bubbling and golden brown. Serve immediately.

Spanakopita Triangles

MAKES: *20 pastries*

PREP TIME: *20 minutes*

COOK TIME: *35 minutes*

SPINACH AND CHEESE FILLING

2 tablespoons (30 mL) unsalted
butter

1 tablespoon (15 mL) extra-virgin
olive oil

4 cloves garlic, minced

1 medium onion, finely diced

Salt and pepper

1 pound (450 g) fresh spinach,
roughly chopped

½ cup (125 mL) fresh parsley,
roughly chopped

1 cup (250 mL) crumbled feta
cheese

1 cup (250 mL) whole-milk
ricotta

2 large eggs, lightly beaten

SPANAKOPITA PASTRY

1 cup (250 mL) unsalted butter

2 cloves garlic, smashed

2 bay leaves

20 sheets filo dough, thawed

While a large spiral spanakopita presents beautifully, these triangles are perfect to serve as an appetizer. They're also much easier to make, as each triangle uses a single sheet of dough folded into a flaky pastry. Be sure to remove as much liquid as possible from the blanched spinach. Any excess water will make the filling soggy.

1. Preheat the oven to 375°F (190°C). Line a baking sheet with parchment paper. Bring a large pot of water to a boil.

2. To make the Spinach and Cheese Filling, in a medium saucepan over medium heat, melt the butter. Add the olive oil and garlic and cook, stirring, for 30 seconds. Add the onion and cook, stirring frequently, until the onion begins to turn translucent, about 5 minutes. Season with salt and pepper.

3. While the onion is cooking, add the spinach to the boiling water and cook until wilted, about 2 minutes. Drain the spinach, rinse with cold water, and squeeze out any excess water. This should yield approximately 1 cup (250 mL) of spinach.

4. Stir the spinach and parsley into the filling. Cook for an additional 2 minutes. Remove from the heat and transfer to a mixing bowl to cool slightly, about 15 minutes. Stir in the feta, ricotta and eggs. Mix well. Set aside while you prepare the pastry.

5. For the Spanakopita Pastry, in a small saucepan over low heat, melt the butter. Add the garlic and bay leaves and cook for 2 minutes. Remove from the heat. Brush a single sheet of filo dough generously with butter. (Keep the remaining sheets covered with a damp tea towel to prevent them drying out.) Fold the dough in half lengthwise, then fold in half lengthwise again so you have a long rectangle. Spoon a tablespoon (15 mL) of filling at one end and fold one corner of the filo over the filling to form a triangle. Continue to fold up the strip, maintaining the triangle shape. Brush the top with additional butter. Place on the prepared baking sheet and cover with a damp tea towel until ready to bake. Repeat until no filling remains.

6. Bake for 20 minutes, or until golden brown.

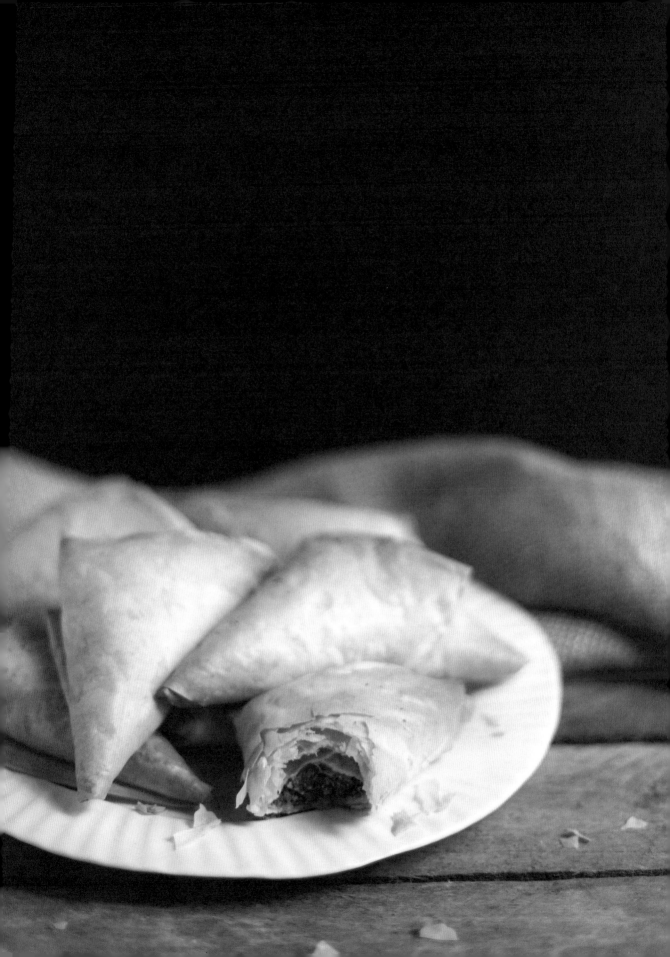

Garlic Scape Brie Biscuits

Garlic scapes are the bud of the garlic plant; think of a garlic-flavoured scallion. Check out your farmers' market in the late spring and early summer to rustle up a bunch, because they aren't available for very long. The subtle garlic flavour complements the creamy Brie cheese in these delicious biscuits. Instead of leaving the Brie in chunks throughout the biscuits, I grate it and work it into the dough, in a similar fashion to the butter.

1. In a large mixing bowl sift the flour, baking powder and salt. Add the Brie and butter. Using a pastry cutter or your hands, work in the Brie and butter until the mixture forms pea-sized crumbs. Fold in the garlic scapes.

2. Add the milk and knead just until the dough comes together. Shape the dough into a disc, wrap in plastic wrap and refrigerate for 1 hour.

3. Preheat the oven to 425°F (220°C). Line a baking sheet with parchment paper.

4. Lightly flour a surface and roll out the dough until ¾ inch (2 cm) thick. Cut into at least 12 rounds using a 2½-inch (6 cm) biscuit cutter. Arrange the biscuits on the prepared baking sheet and brush the tops with cream. This will ensure in a golden brown biscuit.

5. Bake for 15 to 20 minutes, until the tops are golden brown. Let stand for 15 minutes before serving with salted butter.

> **BAKER'S NOTE** Put the Brie in the freezer for 15 minutes before grating. This will firm up the cheese and make it much easier to grate.

MAKES: *12 biscuits*

PREP TIME: *15 minutes*

COOK TIME: *15 minutes*

3 cups (750 mL) all-purpose flour

3½ teaspoons (17 mL) baking powder

1½ teaspoons (7 mL) fine salt

2 cups (500 mL) grated Brie (see Note)

¾ cup (175 mL) unsalted butter, cold and cubed

½ cup (125 mL) thinly sliced garlic scapes

1¼ cups (300 mL) whole milk

1 tablespoon (15 mL) heavy cream

Salted butter, for serving

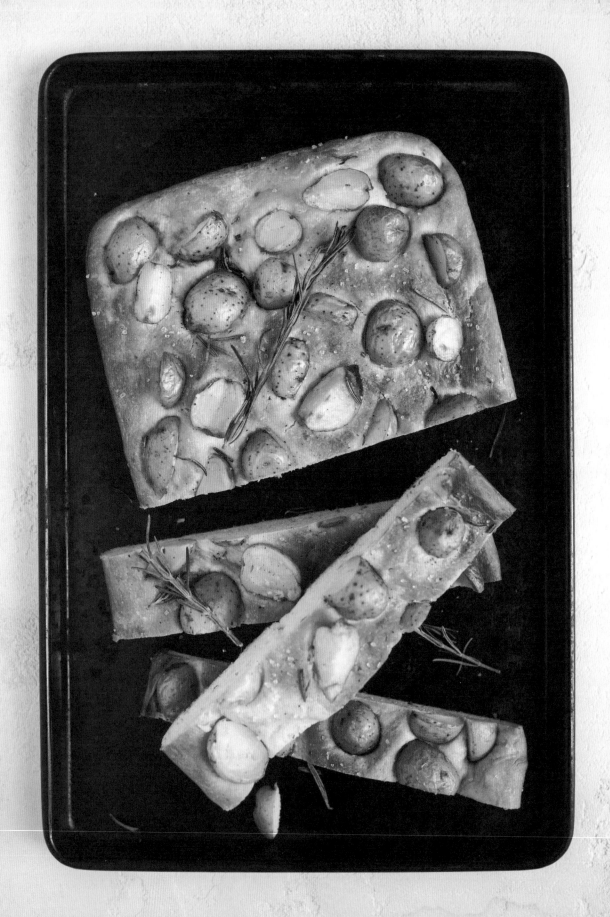

New Potato Rosemary Focaccia

One of my local bakeries sells a delicious potato focaccia, which inspired this recipe. I decided to swap out their thinly sliced potatoes and instead use whole new potatoes. It was everything I'd hoped it would be—a soft focaccia bread base topped with crispy rosemary-infused potatoes. Carb lovers, now you can have the best of both worlds!

SERVES: *8 to 10*

PREP TIME: *75 minutes*

COOK TIME: *50 minutes*

1 cup (250 mL) warm water

1½ teaspoons (7 mL) instant yeast

1 clove garlic, grated

1 tablespoon (15 mL) raw honey

¼ cup (60 mL) + 1 tablespoon (15 mL) extra-virgin olive oil, divided

2 tablespoons (30 mL) roughly chopped fresh rosemary, divided

1 teaspoon (5 mL) fine salt

3 cups (750 mL) all-purpose flour

1 pound (450 g) evenly sized whole new potatoes, halved

1 teaspoon (5 mL) coarse salt

½ teaspoon (2 mL) pepper

1. To the bowl of a stand mixer add the warm water and sprinkle the yeast over top. Let stand for 5 minutes to allow the yeast to activate. If bubbles do not form on the top, start over with fresh yeast.

2. Stir in the garlic, honey, 1 tablespoon (15 mL) of the oil, 1 tablespoon (15 mL) of the rosemary and the fine salt. Fit the mixer with the dough hook. With the mixer on low speed, add the flour 1 cup (250 mL) at a time, mixing until the dough comes together. Knead on medium speed for 8 to 10 minutes. The dough should be smooth and elastic. If it appears too wet, add a touch more flour.

3. On a lightly floured surface, shape the dough into a ball. Place back in the mixer bowl, cover with a damp tea towel and let rest at room temperature until doubled in size, about 1 hour.

4. While the dough rises, in a medium pot, cover the potatoes with cold water and bring to a boil over high heat. Reduce heat to medium and cook for 15 minutes, or until fork-tender. Drain the potatoes and submerge in an ice bath for 1 minute to stop them from cooking any further. Drain again. When cool to the touch, cut them in half. Cut larger potatoes into quarters.

5. Preheat the oven to 400°F (200°C). Brush a 9- x 12-inch (3 L) baking pan or baking sheet with olive oil.

6. Once the dough has risen, punch it down and transfer it to the prepared pan. Press it into the pan, covering as much of the base as you can. Using the tips of your fingers, deeply dimple the dough.

Continues

Evenly scatter the potatoes over the top and press them down into the dough. Brush the top with the remaining ¼ cup (60 mL) oil and sprinkle with the remaining 1 tablespoon (15 mL) rosemary, coarse salt and pepper.

7. Bake for 30 to 35 minutes, until the top is golden brown and the potatoes are crispy. Let cool on the baking sheet for 15 minutes before slicing and serving.

Cheddar and Chive Pretzel Knots

Chives add freshness and brightness to these pretzel knots, which are perfect for an easy grab-and-go snack or served as an appetizer dipped in your favourite sauce. (I always go with classic Dijon mustard.) My mom always has fresh chives in a large swan planter on the back deck. The chives come back every year in the spring and last throughout the summer. To this day I love adding them to just about any savoury baked good for a subtle onion flavour.

MAKES: *20 pretzel knots*

PREP TIME: *75 minutes*

COOK TIME: *25 minutes*

1½ cups (375 mL) warm water

1 package (¼ ounce/8 g) active dry yeast

1 tablespoon (15 mL) turbinado sugar

1 teaspoon (5 mL) fine sea salt

4½ cups (1.125 L) all-purpose flour, divided

6 tablespoons (90 mL) unsalted butter, melted

1½ cups (375 mL) grated mature cheddar cheese, divided

½ cup (125 mL) minced fresh chives

½ cup (125 mL) baking soda

1 egg, whisked, for egg wash

1 tablespoon (15 mL) coarse salt

1. In the bowl of a stand mixer, whisk together the water and yeast. Let stand for 5 minutes to allow the yeast to activate. If bubbles do not form on the top, start over with fresh yeast.

2. Whisk in the sugar and salt. Fit the mixer with the dough hook. With the mixer on low speed, add 1 cup (250 mL) of the flour, followed by the melted butter, mixing until incorporated. Add the remaining flour 1 cup (250 mL) at a time, mixing until the dough comes together. Knead on medium speed for 5 to 7 minutes, until the dough is smooth and elastic. Using your hands, fold in 1 cup (250 mL) of the cheddar and the chives.

3. On a lightly floured surface, shape the dough into a ball. Place back in the mixer bowl, cover with a damp tea towel and let rest at room temperature until doubled in size, about 2 hours.

4. Preheat the oven to 425°F (220°C). Line a baking sheet with parchment paper.

5. Punch down the dough and cut the dough into 20 equal pieces. Using your palms, roll each piece into a 6-inch (15 cm) rope and shape into an overhand knot. Let knots rest covered with a damp kitchen towel while water comes to a boil.

6. In a large pot, bring 8 cups (2 L) water to a boil over high heat. Whisk in the baking soda.

Continues

7. Working in small batches, add pretzels to the boiling water and boil for 30 seconds. Using a slotted spoon, transfer to the prepared baking sheet, spacing them evenly.

8. Brush pretzels with the egg wash. Sprinkle with coarse salt and the remaining ½ cup (125 mL) cheddar.

9. Bake for 15 to 20 minutes, until deep golden brown and doubled in size. Let cool on the baking sheet for 15 minutes. Store in an airtight container at room temperature for up to 2 days or in the freezer for up to 2 weeks.

NIAGARA
BRAND · MARQUE
P.O. BOX 43
VIRGIL, ONTARIO
L0S 1T0

Summer

MY FONDEST summer memories are of spending time with my grandparents. They had the most amazing gardens filled with green beans, peppers, tomatoes, zucchini, eggplant, garlic and so much more. I particularly loved one grandmother's peach tree. It produced the most distinctively flavoured peaches—almost a little sour, but wonderful. We canned these peaches to enjoy throughout the winter months, for snacking and topping pancakes and waffles—which inspired my Peaches and Cream Waffles (page 96). My grandma would also take my sisters and me strawberry picking every summer when the school year ended. We ate just as many strawberries as we picked and spent the afternoon riding around on the back of the farm's tractor. Each summer, I continue to go strawberry picking with Justin. We load up with all kinds of berries when we visit the farm, considering they can be baked into just about anything, from Apricot Raspberry Clafoutis (page 84) to Blueberry Shortcake (page 82) to Blackberry Peach Pie (page 88).

On top of peaches and berries, in this section you'll find recipes featuring zucchini, lavender, tomatoes and fresh herbs. Summer is when farmers' markets are at their best, so take advantage of their offerings! Fresh produce is in abundance, and the possibilities in the kitchen are endless. In the heat of summer we may not want to turn on our ovens, but baking a fresh loaf of Cherry Tomato Focaccia (page 108) or No-Knead Olive Rosemary Bread (page 115) is always worth it. For the dog days of summer, try cooling off with my Raspberry White Chocolate Tart (page 95) or grilling up a Stone Fruit and Prosciutto Pizza (page 118).

Zucchini Pineapple Snack Cake

This recipe brings back so many memories. I grew up eating zucchini bread, which is probably why putting vegetables in a cake has never struck me as odd. We usually enjoy zucchini bread as a snack or a breakfast treat, but here I've turned my aunt's classic recipe into a sheet cake, iced with a thick cream cheese frosting. The cake whips up in one bowl, is easy to transport to a summer barbecue and is even easier to devour. This recipe will become an instant favourite, and your kids won't complain about having to eat vegetables. A slice *does* count as a serving of veggies, right?

1. Preheat the oven to 350°F (180°C). Grease a 9- x 12-inch (3 L) baking pan.

2. In a large mixing bowl combine the eggs, sugar, zucchini, pineapple, oil and vanilla. Stir until evenly blended.

3. Sift in the flour, baking soda, salt, cinnamon and nutmeg. Stir until the batter comes together. Fold in the walnuts, if using.

4. Scrape the batter into the prepared baking pan and bake for 45 to 50 minutes, until the top bounces back when touched or a toothpick inserted in the centre comes out clean. Transfer to a rack and let the cake cool completely while you prepare the frosting.

5. Using an offset spatula, spread the frosting evenly over the cake in a swirling motion. Cut the cake into squares and serve directly from the baking pan.

SERVES: *10 to 12*

PREP TIME: *20 minutes*

COOK TIME: *45 minutes*

3 large eggs

2 cups (500 mL) turbinado sugar

2 cups (500 mL) packed grated zucchini

1 cup (250 mL) canned crushed pineapple, drained

1 cup (250 mL) vegetable oil

2 teaspoons (10 mL) pure vanilla extract

3 cups (750 mL) all-purpose flour

2½ teaspoons (12 mL) baking soda

1 teaspoon (5 mL) fine salt

1 teaspoon (5 mL) cinnamon

½ teaspoon (2 mL) nutmeg

½ cup (125 mL) roughly chopped walnuts (optional)

½ batch Cream Cheese Frosting (page 239)

S'more Cupcakes

MAKES: *12 cupcakes*

PREP TIME: *25 minutes*

COOK TIME: *15 minutes*

GRAHAM CRACKER BASE

1½ cups (375 mL) graham cracker crumbs

3 tablespoons (45 mL) turbinado sugar

Pinch of fine salt

6 tablespoons (90 mL) unsalted butter, melted

CHOCOLATE CAKE

1 cup (250 mL) turbinado sugar

⅓ cup (75 mL) Dutch-processed cocoa powder

1 large egg

½ cup (125 mL) whole milk

½ cup (125 mL) vegetable oil

1 teaspoon (5 mL) vanilla extract

1 cup (250 mL) all-purpose flour

1 teaspoon (5 mL) baking soda

½ teaspoon (2 mL) salt

½ cup (125 mL) boiling water

MARSHMALLOW MERINGUE FROSTING

3 large egg whites, room temperature

¾ cup (175 mL) granulated sugar

1 teaspoon (5 mL) pure vanilla extract

I've come to like s'more desserts more than actual s'mores. They are easier to eat, plus you can enjoy them year-round, since you don't need a campfire to make them. These cupcakes feature each layer of the traditional summer treat: a graham base, a chocolate cake centre and a marshmallow meringue frosting.

1. Preheat the oven to 350°F (180°C). Line a cupcake tin with 12 cupcake liners.

2. To make the Graham Cracker Base, in a small bowl stir together the graham cracker crumbs, sugar, salt and butter. Transfer 2 heaping tablespoons (36 mL) to each cupcake liner and press down to form a bottom crust.

3. To make the Chocolate Cake, in a large mixing bowl whisk together the sugar, cocoa powder, egg, milk, oil and vanilla until well blended. Sift in the flour, baking soda and salt. Mix until combined. Slowly add the boiling water, whisking vigorously.

4. Evenly divide the batter among the cupcake liners. Bake for 15 to 20 minutes, until the tops bounce back when touched or a toothpick inserted in the centre comes out clean. Let cool in the baking pan for 5 minutes then turn the cupcakes out onto a rack to cool completely.

5. While the cupcakes cool, make Marshmallow Meringue Frosting. In a medium saucepan bring 1 inch (2.5 cm) of water to a simmer. In a large heatproof bowl, whisk together the egg whites and sugar until blended. Place over the saucepan, ensuring the bowl does not touch the water, to create a double boiler. Whisk until the sugar is completely dissolved and the egg whites are warm to the touch, about 4 minutes. Immediately transfer the mixture to the bowl of a stand mixer fitted with the whisk attachment. Whisk on medium speed until soft peaks form, about 2 minutes. Add the vanilla and continue whisking until stiff, shiny peaks form, about 4 minutes.

6. Gently transfer the frosting to a piping bag fitted with a large star tip. Pipe the frosting in a circular motion on the top of each cupcake, and lightly brown the meringue using a kitchen torch.

Cherry Streusel Muffins

Years ago, Justin and I decided to have a garage sale to purge some things before we moved. I thought it would be fun to make some muffins to sell, so that people could snack while they browsed. In the end, the garage sale was a complete bust, but the neighbourhood went crazy over my blueberry streusel muffins! As always, the baked goods prevailed. This recipe is a cherry twist on the original.

1. Preheat the oven to 350°F (180°C). Line a muffin tin with 12 muffin liners.

2. To make the Streusel Topping, in a medium mixing bowl combine the flour, sugar, salt, cinnamon, nutmeg, butter and vanilla. Using your hands, work the butter into the dry ingredients until the mixture forms crumbs. Set aside while you prepare the muffins.

3. To make the Muffins, in a large mixing bowl whisk together the eggs, sugar, yogurt, butter, oil and vanilla, about 2 minutes. Sift in the flour, baking powder, salt, cinnamon and nutmeg. Stir until the flour is just combined. Gently fold in the cherries. Evenly distribute the batter among the muffin liners. Top with the streusel.

4. Bake for 20 to 25 minutes, until the tops bounce back when touched or until a toothpick inserted in the centre comes out clean. Let cool in the tin for 15 minutes before turning out onto a rack to cool completely. Store in an airtight container at room temperature for up to 2 days.

BAKER'S NOTE If you would like to try out the original blueberry streusel muffins, replace the cherries with 2 cups (500 mL) fresh blueberries.

MAKES: *12 muffins*

PREP TIME: *15 minutes*

COOK TIME: *20 minutes*

STREUSEL TOPPING

1 cup (250 mL) all-purpose flour

¾ cup (175 mL) turbinado sugar

¼ teaspoon (1 mL) fine salt

½ teaspoon (2 mL) cinnamon

Pinch of nutmeg

4 tablespoons (60 mL) unsalted butter, cold and cubed

1 teaspoon (5 mL) pure vanilla extract

MUFFINS

2 large eggs

1 cup (250 mL) turbinado sugar

¾ cup (175 mL) plain or vanilla full-fat yogurt

4 tablespoons (60 mL) unsalted butter, melted

¼ cup (60 mL) vegetable oil

1 teaspoon (5 mL) pure vanilla extract

2½ cups (625 mL) all-purpose flour

2 teaspoons (10 mL) baking powder

½ teaspoon (2 mL) fine salt

½ teaspoon (2 mL) cinnamon

¼ teaspoon (1 mL) nutmeg

2 cups (500 mL) pitted sweet cherries, roughly chopped

Chamomile Blueberry Scones

MAKES: *8 scones*

PREP TIME: *15 minutes*

COOK TIME: *25 minutes*

¾ cup (175 mL) heavy cream, plus more for brushing

1 chamomile tea bag

2¼ cups (550 mL) all-purpose flour

½ cup (125 mL) turbinado sugar, plus more for sprinkling

1 teaspoon (5 mL) baking powder

½ teaspoon (2 mL) baking soda

½ teaspoon (2 mL) fine salt

½ cup (125 mL) unsalted butter, cold and cubed

1 large egg, lightly beaten

1 teaspoon (5 mL) pure vanilla extract

1 cup (250 mL) fresh blueberries

Scones are often enjoyed alongside a cup of hot tea, and I play on that tradition here. These scones feature a hint of chamomile flavour from steeping the tea in the cream. I recommend using a fresh, quality tea for maximum flavour; my go-to for chamomile tea is Steven Smith Teamaker's No. 67 Meadow blend. I love these scones' combination of slight flowery notes from the chamomile and juicy, bursting-sweet blueberries.

1. Preheat the oven to 400°F (200°C). Line a baking sheet with parchment paper.

2. In a small saucepan over low heat combine the cream and chamomile tea bag. Bring to a simmer, then remove from the heat and let steep for 5 to 10 minutes. Discard the tea bag and set aside the infused cream to cool.

3. In a large mixing bowl sift the flour, sugar, baking powder, baking soda and salt. Add the butter. Using your hands or a pastry cutter, work in the butter until the mixture resembles pea-sized crumbs. Add the egg, vanilla and cooled cream. Stir just until the dough comes together. Fold in the blueberries.

4. Transfer the dough to a lightly floured surface. Using your hands or a rolling pin, shape into a disc 1 to 1½ inches (2.5 to 4 cm) thick. Cut into 8 even wedges. Arrange wedges on the prepared baking sheet, brush the tops with cream. Sprinkle with sugar, if desired.

5. Bake for 20 minutes, or until the tops are golden brown. Let cool for 15 minutes on a rack before serving.

Lemon Lavender Shortbread

I love incorporating less-common flavours into my baked goods. We often associate lavender with the calming scents of soaps and candles, but it tastes amazing in a dessert, too! Here, lavender and lemon zest really brighten the flavour of the shortbread. The subtle flavours make this shortbread and a hot cup of tea the perfect pairing. In the summer, Niagara-on-the-Lake has the most beautiful lavender festival. Each year I pick up a bouquet of fresh lavender and a little jar of freshly dried culinary lavender.

1. Preheat the oven to 350°F (180°C). Line 2 baking sheets with parchment paper.

2. In the bowl of a stand mixer fitted with the paddle attachment, combine the sugar, butter, lavender, lemon zest, and vanilla. Beat on medium speed until fluffy.

3. Sift in the flour and salt. Beat just until the dough comes together. If the dough appears dry, beat in a tablespoon (15 mL) of ice water at a time until you can press it together.

4. On a lightly floured surface, roll out dough to ½-inch (1 cm) thickness. Cut out 24 rounds with a 2½-inch (6 cm) cookie cutter and arrange 12 rounds on each prepared baking sheet.

5. Bake for 8 to 10 minutes, until the edges are lightly browned. Transfer the cookies to a rack and let cool for at least 10 minutes before eating. Store in an airtight container at room temperature for up to 2 days.

BAKER'S NOTE You can find culinary lavender in specialty spice stores, higher-end grocery stores and online.

MAKES: *24 cookies*

PREP TIME: *15 minutes*

COOK TIME: *8 minutes*

1 cup (250 mL) turbinado sugar

¾ cup (175 mL) unsalted butter, room temperature

1 teaspoon (5 mL) culinary lavender

1 teaspoon (5 mL) grated lemon zest

1 teaspoon (5 mL) pure vanilla extract

3 cups (750 mL) all-purpose flour

½ teaspoon (2 mL) fine salt

1 to 2 tablespoons (15 to 30 mL) ice water

S'more Brownies

SERVES: *10 to 12*

PREP TIME: *15 minutes*

COOK TIME: *30 minutes*

GRAHAM CRACKER BASE

1½ cups (375 mL) graham
cracker crumbs

3 tablespoons (45 mL) turbinado
sugar

Pinch of fine salt

6 tablespoons (90 mL) unsalted
butter, melted

S'MORE BROWNIE BATTER

2 large eggs

1 cup (250 mL) turbinado sugar

¾ cup (175 mL) Dutch-processed
cocoa powder

¾ cup (175 mL) unsalted butter,
melted

1 teaspoon (5 mL) pure vanilla
extract

½ cup (125 mL) all-purpose flour

½ teaspoon (2 mL) fine salt

1 cup (250 mL) mini
marshmallows

¼ cup (60 mL) milk chocolate
chunks

S'mores might just be one of the best parts of summer, but you don't need a campfire to make these epic brownies! I love the graham cracker base, which elevates the flavour of this classic treat. Take these to the next level by serving them with vanilla ice cream and fudge sauce.

1. Preheat the oven to 350°F (180°C). Line the bottom and sides of an 8-inch (20 cm) square baking dish with parchment paper.

2. To make the Graham Cracker Base, in a small bowl stir together the graham cracker crumbs, sugar, salt and butter. Transfer to the prepared baking dish and press down to form an even crust.

3. To make the Brownie Batter, in a medium mixing bowl combine the eggs, sugar, cocoa powder, butter and vanilla. Whisk until well blended. Sift in the flour and salt, and mix until combined. Pour the batter over the graham cracker base. Top with the marshmallows and chocolate chunks.

4. Bake for 30 to 35 minutes, until the marshmallows are golden brown. (When it comes to a brownie, a little undercooked is okay.) Let cool completely before removing from the pan and slicing.

Blueberry Shortcake

SERVES: *8 to 10*

PREP TIME: *20 minutes*

COOK TIME: *25 minutes*

CHIFFON CAKE

4 large eggs, separated

1 cup (250 mL) turbinado sugar

¼ cup (60 mL) vegetable oil

4 tablespoons (60 mL) unsalted
butter, melted

2 teaspoons (10 mL) pure vanilla
extract

1½ cups (375 mL) all-purpose
flour

2 teaspoons (10 mL) baking
powder

½ teaspoon (2 mL) fine salt

½ cup (125 mL) whole milk

FILLING

2 batches Fresh Whipped Cream
(page 240)

4 cups (1 L) fresh blueberries

Strawberry shortcake is my favourite dessert, so the idea of making it with blueberries piqued my interest. If you're making this cake a day in advance, I suggest brushing each cake layer with Vanilla Simple Syrup (page 240) to prevent the chiffon cake from drying. I recommend serving this cake the same day it's assembled, as chiffon cake and fresh whipped cream are delicate and best enjoyed fresh. And if you're a *Gilmore Girls* fan, this one's for you.

1. Preheat the oven to 350°F (180°C). Grease and line the bottom of two 8-inch (20 cm) round cake pans with parchment paper. Grease the sides.

2. To make the Chiffon Cake, in a large mixing bowl combine the egg yolks, sugar, oil, butter and vanilla. Whisk until smooth.

3. In a medium mixing bowl beat the egg whites until stiff peaks form.

4. Sift the flour, baking powder and salt into the cake batter. Stir until just combined. Add the milk and stir just until smooth. Gently fold in the egg whites, being careful not to deflate them.

5. Divide the batter between the prepared cake pans and bake for 25 to 30 minutes, until the cake bounces back when touched or a toothpick inserted in the centre comes out clean. Transfer to racks and let cool completely before removing from the pans.

6. Once the cakes have cooled, use a long serrated knife to score the entire outside edge of each cake halfway up the side. Using this line as a guide, carefully cut through each cake to create 4 layers.

7. Place the first layer of cake on a cake stand and top with 1 cup (250 mL) of the whipped cream. Sprinkle evenly with 1 cup (250 mL) of the blueberries. Repeat, ending with a final layer of whipped cream and blueberries. Serve immediately.

Apricot Raspberry Clafoutis

SERVES: *4 to 6*

PREP TIME: *45 minutes*

COOK TIME: *55 minutes*

¾ cup (175 mL) heavy cream

½ cup (125 mL) whole milk

1 teaspoon (5 mL) pure vanilla extract

3 large eggs

½ cup (125 mL) turbinado sugar

½ cup (125 mL) all-purpose flour

¼ teaspoon (1 mL) fine salt

¼ teaspoon (1 mL) nutmeg

1 cup (250 mL) raspberries, plus more for serving

6 apricots, halved and pitted, plus more for serving

Icing sugar, for dusting

This classic French summer treat is made by pouring an egg-based batter over fruit and baking until golden brown. Clafoutis is typically made with fresh sweet cherries, but I find it works well with any fresh summer fruit, which allows you to get creative with whatever's fresh and ripe at the market. I love the colour combination of the raspberries and apricots. This simple clafoutis will definitely be a hit at your next outdoor gathering!

1. Preheat the oven to 375°F (190°C). Grease a 9-inch (23 cm) round baking dish.

2. In a blender combine the cream, milk, vanilla, eggs, sugar, flour, salt and nutmeg. Blend until smooth. Let the batter rest for 30 minutes at room temperature.

3. Pour one-third of the batter into the prepared baking dish. Bake for 15 minutes.

4. Remove from the oven and evenly distribute the raspberries and apricots over the batter. Pour the remaining batter over the fruit and bake for an additional 40 to 45 minutes, until the clafoutis is slightly puffed and the top is golden.

5. Before serving, sprinkle generously with icing sugar and top with additional fresh fruit, if desired.

Peach Basil Crumble

In the summer my mom grows the most amazing herbs, but nothing beats her basil plant. She constantly brings me bunches, which is good because I can never get enough. While my mom mainly uses it in savoury dishes, I can't help but incorporate it into my desserts. There is something about the flavour combination of peaches and basil that confirms that they were made for each other. The sweetness of the fruit and the herbaceous freshness of the basil complement each other perfectly.

1. Preheat the oven to 350°F (180°C).

2. To make the Peach Basil Filling, in a large mixing bowl combine the peaches, sugar, cornstarch, vanilla and basil. Toss to coat. Pour into a 9- x 12-inch (3 L) baking dish and set aside while you prepare the topping.

3. To make the Crumble Topping, in a large mixing bowl combine the oats, flour, sugar, walnuts, salt and nutmeg. Stir until evenly mixed. Add the cubed butter. Using your hands, work the butter into the oat mixture until a crumbly mixture is formed. Evenly disperse the crumble over the peaches.

4. Bake for 45 to 50 minutes, until the crumble is golden brown and the fruit filling is bubbling. Let cool for 15 minutes before serving. Serve warm with vanilla ice cream or Fresh Whipped Cream.

SERVES: *6 to 8*

PREP TIME: *20 minutes*

COOK TIME: *45 minutes*

PEACH BASIL FILLING

8 to 10 ripe peaches, pitted and sliced

½ cup (125 mL) turbinado sugar

2 tablespoons (30 mL) cornstarch

1 teaspoon (5 mL) pure vanilla extract

¼ cup (60 mL) finely chopped fresh basil

CRUMBLE TOPPING

1 cup (250 mL) old-fashioned rolled oats

¾ cup (175 mL) all-purpose flour

¾ cup (175 mL) turbinado sugar

½ cup (125 mL) walnuts, roughly chopped

½ teaspoon (2 mL) fine salt

Pinch of nutmeg

½ cup (125 mL) unsalted butter, cold and cubed

FOR SERVING

Vanilla ice cream or Fresh Whipped Cream (page 240)

Blackberry Peach Pie

SERVES: *6 to 8*

PREP TIME: *45 minutes*

COOK TIME: *60 minutes*

4 cups (1 L) pitted and sliced ripe
peaches

2 cups (500 mL) fresh
blackberries

¾ cup (175 mL) turbinado sugar,
plus extra for sprinkling

3 tablespoons (45 mL) cornstarch

1½ teaspoons (7 mL) fresh lemon
juice

1 teaspoon (5 mL) pure vanilla
extract

¼ teaspoon (1 mL) cinnamon

¼ teaspoon (1 mL) nutmeg

1 batch Double Pie Dough
(page 243), chilled

1 egg, whisked, for egg wash

I am a strong believer in "if it grows together, it goes together." Mixing the best of summer stone fruit with fresh summer berries is a perfect pie pairing. Blackberries were the first things we planted when we moved into our home (and may or may not be the only thing that lived). While it will be years before I will be getting pounds and pounds of blackberries to make batches of fresh jam, we get enough during the summer season to whip up a pie or two. This blackberry peach pie is my go-to recipe!

1. Preheat the oven to 400°F (200°C).

2. In a large mixing bowl combine the peaches, blackberries, sugar, cornstarch, lemon juice, vanilla, cinnamon and nutmeg. Toss to coat.

3. On a lightly floured surface, roll out half the pie dough until ¼ inch (5 mm) thick. Gently lift and transfer the dough to a 9-inch (23 cm) round pie plate. Gently press the dough into the bottom and sides of the plate. Spoon in the fruit filling.

4. To make the lattice top, roll out the remaining pie dough to ¼-inch (5 mm) thickness. Using a pastry cutter, cut the dough into strips ½ inch (1 cm) wide. Evenly lay 5 strips vertically over the filling. Fold back every other strip halfway. Place another strip horizontally across the filling, right next to the folds, and unfold the folded strips over it. Fold back the opposite vertical strips and place a second strip of dough horizontally across the filling, about ½ inch (1 cm) from the first horizontal strip. Unfold the folded strips over the horizontal strip. Repeat on both halves of the pie until the weave is complete. Trim the edges of the strips, leaving a ½-inch (1 cm) overhang. Fold under the overhang, then crimp edges. To crimp the edges, place an index finger on the lip of the pie plate and pinch around that finger with the index finger and thumb of your other hand, holding the dough in between.

5. Brush the dough with the egg wash and sprinkle with additional sugar, if desired. Chill the pie chill for 30 minutes.

6. Bake for 60 minutes, or until the top is golden and the fruit is bubbling. If the top begins to brown too quickly, tent with foil. Let cool completely before serving.

Cherry Hand Pies

There is something so cute about serving individual-sized dishes and desserts. I love that they're perfectly portioned and easy to serve. Plus, you get to eat the *whole* pie to yourself without any judgment! These pies feature the sweetest of sweet cherries and an all-shortening crust to maximize flakiness. Just try not to eat all the cherry filling with a spoon before it makes it into the pies . . . I speak from experience.

1. To make the Hand Pie Pastry, in a large mixing bowl sift the flour, sugar and salt. Add the shortening. Using a pastry cutter or your hands, work shortening into the dough until the mixture forms pea-sized crumbs. Add the ice water and vanilla and toss gently until the dough comes together. Shape the dough into a disc, wrap in plastic wrap and chill for 1 hour while you make the filling.

2. To make the Cherry Filling, in a large saucepan combine the cherries, sugar, cornstarch, vanilla and lemon juice. Cook over medium heat until the cherries begin to break down, 5 to 8 minutes. Set aside to cool to room temperature (otherwise it will melt the dough).

3. Preheat the oven to 350°F (180°C). Line 2 baking sheets with parchment paper.

4. To assemble the hand pies, on a lightly floured surface roll out the dough until ¼ inch (5 mm) thick. Cut out 24 rounds with a 4-inch (10 cm) cookie cutter.

5. Spoon 1 tablespoon (15 mL) Cherry Filling onto the centre of a dough round. Brush the edges with egg wash and top with a second pastry round. Press the edges with a fork to seal and score the top with a small sharp knife to allow steam to escape. Repeat with the remaining dough rounds, arranging 6 pies on each prepared baking sheet. Brush the tops with egg wash and sprinkle with turbinado sugar.

6. Bake for 20 to 25 minutes, until the filling is bubbling and the tops are golden. Let cool on a rack for at least 15 minutes before serving. Store in an airtight container at room temperature for up to 2 days.

MAKES: *12 hand pies*

PREP TIME: *20 minutes*

COOK TIME: *30 minutes*

HAND PIE PASTRY

2 cups (500 mL) all-purpose flour

2 tablespoons (30 mL) granulated sugar

⅛ teaspoon (0.5 mL) fine salt

¾ cup (175 mL) vegetable shortening, cold

½ cup (125 mL) ice water

1 teaspoon (5 mL) pure vanilla extract

1 tablespoon (15 mL) turbinado sugar, for sprinkling

CHERRY FILLING

3 cups (750 mL) pitted and halved sweet cherries

½ cup (125 mL) turbinado sugar

2 tablespoons (30 mL) cornstarch

1 teaspoon (5 mL) pure vanilla extract

1 teaspoon (5 mL) fresh lemon juice

1 egg, whisked, for egg wash

Plum Galette ———————

SERVES: *6 to 8*

PREP TIME: *20 minutes*

COOK TIME: *45 minutes*

8 to 10 ripe plums, pitted and sliced

½ cup (125 mL) turbinado sugar

1 tablespoon (15 mL) cornstarch

¼ teaspoon (1 mL) cinnamon

1½ teaspoons (7 mL) fresh lemon juice

1 teaspoon (5 mL) pure vanilla extract

1 batch Single Pie Dough (page 243), chilled

1 egg, whisked, for egg wash

Galettes are much simpler to make than pies, and their rustic look is what makes them beautiful. You don't have to worry about creating the perfect lattice top or perfectly crimping the edges. If you are new to pie making, I strongly suggest starting with this easy plum galette recipe. It will ease any pie-making fears you might have as well as give plums their moment to shine this season!

1. Preheat the oven to 375°F (190°C). Line a baking sheet with parchment paper.

2. In a large mixing bowl combine the plums, sugar, cornstarch, cinnamon, lemon juice and vanilla. Toss to coat.

3. On a lightly floured surface, roll out the chilled pie dough into a circle ¼ inch (5 mm) thick. It doesn't have to be a perfect circle. Carefully transfer the dough to the prepared baking sheet.

4. Arrange the plums in a circular pattern over the pastry, layering the plums as you go and leaving a 1-inch (2.5 cm) border. Gently fold the dough border over, pleating it as needed, and brush with the egg wash. Chill the galette for 15 minutes.

5. Bake for 45 to 50 minutes, until the crust browns and the fruit filling is bubbling. Serve warm or at room temperature.

Raspberry White Chocolate Tart

When it comes to chocolate, there seems to be a 50-50 split between people who love white chocolate and people who hate it. I fall into the love category. I was the kid who always received the white chocolate Easter bunny. This pie is a white chocolate twist on a classic chocolate pie. It is rich, creamy and full of the sweet white chocolate flavour we all (or half of us) love, and makes a lovely addition to any summer celebration. The fresh raspberries on top add a little tartness to offset the sweetness of the filling. It is very important to use a quality white chocolate in this pie, as it will provide the best flavour.

1. Make the Graham Cracker Pie Crust, using a 9-inch (23 cm) pie plate and bake as directed. Let cool.

2. In a large saucepan whisk together the egg yolks, milk, cream, sugar, cornstarch and salt; whisk until blended. Simmer over medium heat, constantly stirring, until the mixture bubbles and thickens, about 10 minutes.

3. Once the mixture has thickened, remove from heat and add 8 ounces (225 g) of the white chocolate, the butter and vanilla. Stir until the chocolate and butter have melted and the mixture is smooth. Pour the mixture into the cooled pie crust. Let the pie set for 4 to 6 hours in the refrigerator.

4. Before serving, in a small microwave-safe bowl, melt the remaining 2 ounces (55 g) white chocolate in the microwave in 15-second increments, stirring after each increment, until fully melted. Top the pie with fresh raspberries and drizzle with the melted white chocolate.

SERVES: *6 to 8*

PREP TIME: *2 hours*

COOK TIME: *15 minutes*

1 batch Graham Cracker Pie Crust (page 31)

4 large egg yolks

2 cups (500 mL) whole milk

1 cup (250 mL) heavy cream

1½ cups (375 mL) turbinado sugar

¼ cup (60 mL) cornstarch

½ teaspoon (2 mL) fine salt

10 ounces (280 g) quality white chocolate, roughly chopped, divided

3 tablespoons (45 mL) unsalted butter, cubed

2 teaspoons (10 mL) pure vanilla extract

2 cups (500 mL) fresh raspberries, for topping

Peaches and Cream Waffles

MAKES: *6 Belgian waffles*

PREP TIME: *10 minutes*

COOK TIME: *15 minutes*

2 large eggs, separated

1¼ cups (300 mL) whole milk

½ cup (125 mL) vanilla or plain
full-fat yogurt

¼ cup (60 mL) turbinado sugar

3 tablespoons (45 mL) unsalted
butter, melted

1 teaspoon (5 mL) pure vanilla
extract

2 cups (500 mL) all-purpose flour

2 tablespoons (30 mL) cornstarch

1 tablespoon (15 mL) baking
powder

Pinch of fine salt

Pinch of nutmeg

2 cups (500 mL) thinly sliced
peaches

Pure maple syrup, for serving

Fresh Whipped Cream
(page 240), for serving

This recipe was inspired by one of my favourite breakfast memories when I was growing up. In the summer months, my grandparents would can dozens of mason jars full of fresh peaches, and then on Sunday mornings, my mom would make us fresh waffles and we would pile them high with those sweet peaches. Waffles really are what weekend mornings are all about. And don't forget the maple syrup and whipped cream!

1. In a large mixing bowl combine the egg yolks, milk, yogurt, sugar, butter and vanilla. Whisk until well blended. Sift in the flour, cornstarch, baking powder, salt and nutmeg. Mix until just combined.

2. In a medium mixing bowl whisk the egg whites to stiff peaks. Gently fold them into the batter, being careful not to deflate the whites.

3. Preheat and grease a nonstick waffle iron. Cook the waffles according to your iron's directions for about 4 to 6 minutes, or until crispy and golden brown.

4. Plate the waffles and top with sliced peaches. Serve with maple syrup and whipped cream.

Heirloom Tomato Galette

SERVES: *6 to 8*

PREP TIME: *15 minutes*

COOK TIME: *45 minutes*

1 batch Single Pie Dough
   (page 243), chilled

⅓ cup (75 mL) basil pesto,
   homemade or store-bought

½ cup (125 mL) thinly sliced
   fresh mozzarella cheese

2 cups (500 mL) mixed heirloom
   cherry tomatoes, halved

2 tablespoons (30 mL) extra-
   virgin olive oil

Pinch of fine salt

Pinch of freshly ground pepper

1 egg, whisked, for egg wash

¼ cup (60 mL) freshly grated
   Parmesan cheese

Sun-ripened tomatoes are my favourite thing about the late summer. They taste so fresh and sweet. I remember my grandma slicing up tomatoes from her garden, drizzling them generously with olive oil and sprinkling with sea salt, to serve to us as the perfect snack. Sometimes the simplest things in life are the best. Maybe it's the Italian in me, but I can't help but love every variety of tomato. This galette combines a rainbow of heirloom tomatoes, but regular red cherry tomatoes will do the trick.

1. Preheat the oven to 375°F (190°C). Line a baking sheet with parchment paper.

2. On a lightly floured surface, roll out the pie dough into a circle that is ¼ inch (5 mm) thick. Gently lift and transfer the dough to the prepared baking sheet.

3. Brush the dough with the pesto, leaving a 1-inch (2.5 cm) border. Layer the mozzarella over the pesto.

4. In a large mixing bowl toss together the tomatoes, oil, salt and pepper. Spread the tomatoes over the cheese. Gently fold the dough border over, pleating it as needed. Brush dough with the egg wash and sprinkle the edges with the Parmesan.

5. Bake for 45 to 50 minutes, until the crust is golden brown and the tomatoes burst. Serve immediately.

Ratatouille Gratin

SERVES: *6 to 8*

PREP TIME: *20 minutes*

COOK TIME: *60 minutes*

VEGETABLE LAYER

1 zucchini, thinly sliced

1 small yellow squash, thinly sliced

1 small eggplant, thinly sliced

3 Roma tomatoes, thinly sliced

1 teaspoon (5 mL) fine salt

2 tablespoons (30 mL) extra-virgin olive oil

2 cloves garlic, minced

1 teaspoon (5 mL) chopped fresh thyme

Freshly ground black pepper

ONION LAYER

2 tablespoons (30 mL) unsalted butter

2 tablespoons (30 mL) extra-virgin olive oil

2 cloves garlic, minced

2 medium onions, thinly sliced

1 teaspoon (5 mL) chopped fresh thyme

Salt and pepper

GRATIN TOPPING

1 cup (250 mL) freshly grated Parmesan cheese

1 cup (250 mL) panko breadcrumbs

2 tablespoons (30 mL) extra-virgin olive oil

1 teaspoon (5 mL) chopped fresh thyme

Salt and pepper

This gratin is a baked twist on ratatouille. It features a wonderful variety of fresh late-summer produce as well as the ingredients you would find in a traditional ratatouille. The colours are so vibrant that even those who refuse to eat their vegetables won't be able to resist this dish!

1. For the Vegetable Layer, in a large mixing bowl combine the zucchini, yellow squash, eggplant and tomatoes. Sprinkle with the salt and toss to coat. Let the vegetables sit for 15 minutes to allow the salt to drain out any excess water. Drain the vegetables in a colander, then return them to the bowl and add the oil, garlic, thyme and pepper to taste. Toss well. Add more salt, if desired. Set aside.

2. For the Onion Layer, in a large skillet over medium heat, melt the butter. Add the oil and garlic and cook, stirring, until the garlic is fragrant, about 30 seconds. Add the onions, thyme, and salt and pepper to taste. Cook, stirring often, until the onions are translucent and soft but not caramelized, about 10 minutes. Remove from the heat.

3. Preheat the oven to 350°F (180°C).

4. Evenly spread half the cooked onions in a medium casserole dish. Top with half the vegetables, spreading evenly. Spread the remaining onions over the vegetables and top with a final layer of the vegetables.

5. To make the Gratin Topping, in a small bowl combine the Parmesan, panko, oil, thyme, and salt and pepper to taste. Spread the topping over the layered vegetables.

6. Bake for 45 minutes, or until the vegetables are cooked through and the top is golden brown. Serve warm.

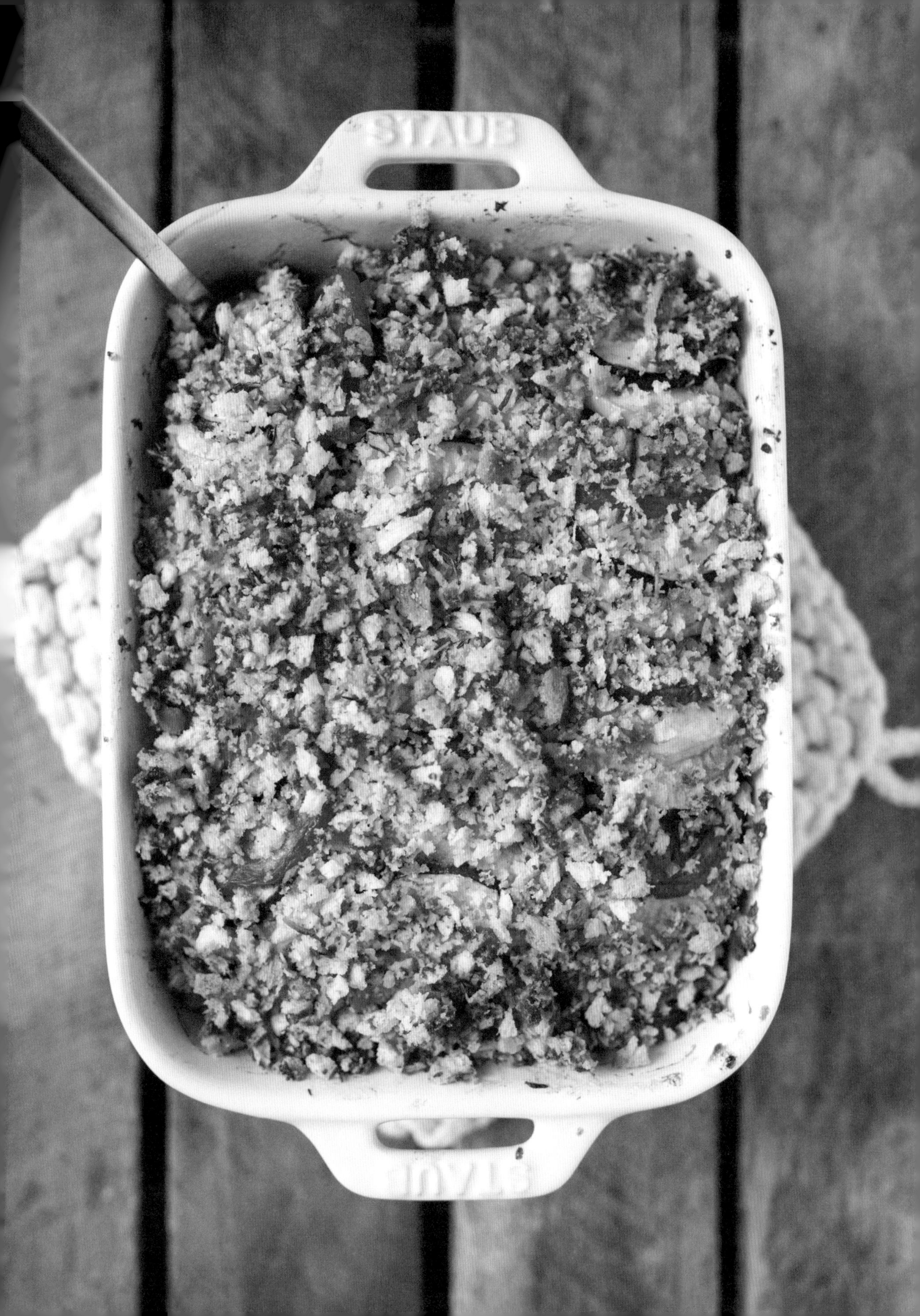

Tomato Basil Turnovers

These turnovers are inspired by the flavours of a Margherita pizza and are so simple to make. When you bite into the puff pastry, you'll instantly be transported to summer, or at least an Italian summer. I love to make these with basil and tomatoes picked straight from my mom's garden, but considering not everyone has a garden at home, check out your local farmers' market for the freshest ingredients you can find.

1. Preheat the oven to 375°F (190°C). Line a baking sheet with parchment paper.

2. On a lightly floured surface, roll out each sheet of puff pastry into a 6- x 9-inch (16 x 24 cm) rectangle. Cut each sheet into six 3-inch (8 cm) squares. In the centre of each square, place a slice of mozzarella, a basil leaf and a tomato slice. Drizzle each tomato slice with some of the olive oil and season with salt and pepper.

3. Fold two of the edges over the filling and pinch together to seal. Brush the pastry with the egg wash and transfer to the prepared baking sheet.

4. Bake for 20 to 25 minutes, until golden brown. Serve warm.

MAKES: *12 turnovers*

PREP TIME: *15 minutes*

COOK TIME: *20 minutes*

2 sheets (16 ounces/450 g) frozen all-butter puff pastry, thawed

4 ounces (115 g) fresh mozzarella cheese, cut into 12 thin slices

12 whole basil leaves

2 large tomatoes, halved and cut into 12 slices

1 tablespoon (15 mL) extra-virgin olive oil

Salt and pepper

1 egg, whisked, for egg wash

Sun-Dried Tomato and Asiago Scones

MAKES: *8 scones*

PREP TIME: *15 minutes*

COOK TIME: *15 minutes*

2¼ cups (550 mL) all-purpose flour

1 tablespoon (15 mL) turbinado sugar

1 tablespoon (15 mL) baking powder

1 teaspoon (5 mL) fine salt

½ cup (125 mL) unsalted butter, cold and cubed

1 cup (250 mL) grated Asiago cheese

2 large eggs

¾ cup (175 mL) whole milk

¼ cup (60 mL) + 2 tablespoons (30 mL) heavy cream, divided

½ cup (125 mL) dry-packed sun-dried tomatoes, roughly chopped

Asiago is one of my favourite cheeses, and I love its strong flavour in baked goods. The sweetness of the sun-dried tomatoes balances out the saltiness of the Asiago in these scones. They are perfect for breakfast, lunch or an afternoon snack.

1. Preheat the oven to 400°F (200°C). Line a baking sheet with parchment paper.

2. In a large mixing bowl whisk together the flour, sugar, baking powder and salt. Add the butter and cheese. Using your hands, work in the butter until the mixture forms pea-sized crumbs.

3. In a small bowl whisk together the eggs, milk and ¼ cup (60 mL) of the cream. Add the wet ingredients to the crumb mixture and stir until the dough comes together. Fold in the sun-dried tomatoes.

4. Turn the dough out onto a lightly floured surface and shape into a disc ¾ inch (2 cm) thick. Cut into 8 even wedges. Arrange wedges on the prepared baking sheet and brush the tops with the remaining 2 tablespoons (30 mL) cream.

5. Bake for 15 to 20 minutes, until the scones have puffed and are golden brown. Let cool on a rack for 15 minutes before serving. Store in an airtight container in the refrigerator for up to 2 days or for 2 weeks in the freezer.

Herb and Gorgonzola Muffins

This is a muffin for all you savoury breakfast lovers like myself. As much as I love a chocolate chunk muffin with my coffee, I'm not always in the mood for dessert for breakfast. This muffin can be enjoyed dipped in a runny egg or with a generous smear of butter. The taste is similar to a biscuit, but the texture is light and fluffy. The Gorgonzola cheese adds a punch of flavour, but this recipe will work with any flavourful cheese you have on hand.

1. Preheat the oven to 375°F (190°C). Line a muffin tin with 12 muffin liners.

2. In a medium mixing bowl whisk together the eggs, garlic, milk, butter and parsley until well combined. Sift in the flour, baking powder, salt and pepper. Stir just until the batter comes together, then fold in the Gorgonzola cheese.

3. Evenly divide the batter among the prepared muffin liners. Sprinkle with a touch of fresh parsley, if desired. Bake for 20 minutes, or until the tops are golden brown or a toothpick inserted in the centre comes out clean. Let rest in the pan for 15 minutes and serve warm with butter. Store in an airtight container for up to 48 hours.

MAKES: *12 muffins*

PREP TIME: *15 minutes*

COOK TIME: *20 minutes*

2 large eggs

1 clove garlic, minced

1 cup (250 mL) whole milk

8 tablespoons (125 mL) unsalted butter, melted

¼ cup (60 mL) roughly chopped fresh parsley, plus more for sprinkling

1½ cups (375 mL) all-purpose flour

2½ teaspoons (12 mL) baking powder

½ teaspoon (2 mL) salt

½ teaspoon (2 mL) pepper

¾ cup (175 mL) crumbled Gorgonzola cheese

Cherry Tomato Focaccia

SERVES: *8 to 10*

PREP TIME: *2 hours*

COOK TIME: *30 minutes*

1½ cups (375 mL) warm water

1 package (¼ ounce/8 g) instant yeast

2 cloves garlic, grated

2 tablespoons (30 mL) raw honey

4 tablespoons (60 mL) extra-virgin olive oil, divided

1½ teaspoons (7 mL) fine salt

4½ cups (1.125 L) all-purpose flour

1 cup (250 mL) halved cherry tomatoes

1 tablespoon (15 mL) chopped fresh oregano

1 teaspoon (5 mL) coarse sea salt

Freshly ground black pepper

While I love roasting cherry tomatoes for a charcuterie board or pasta dishes, or slathering them on fresh bread, cherry tomato focaccia will always be my favourite way to use them. Fresh oregano is my herb of choice for this bread (don't use dried). It shines through and complements the sweet sun-ripened tomatoes.

1. To the bowl of a stand mixer add the warm water and sprinkle the yeast over top. Let stand for 5 minutes to allow the yeast to activate. If bubbles do not form on the top, start over with fresh yeast.

2. Stir in the garlic, honey, 2 tablespoons (30 mL) of the oil and the fine salt. Fit the mixer with the dough hook. With the mixer on low speed, add the flour 1 cup (250 mL) at a time, mixing until the dough comes together. Knead on medium speed for 8 to 10 minutes. The dough should be smooth and elastic. If it appears too wet, add a touch more flour.

3. On a lightly floured surface, shape the dough into a ball. Place back in the mixer bowl, cover with a damp tea towel and let rest at room temperature until doubled in size, about 1 hour.

4. Preheat the oven to 400°F (200°C). Brush a 9- x 12-inch (3 L) baking pan or baking sheet with olive oil.

5. Once the dough has risen, punch it down and transfer it to the prepared pan. Press it into the pan, covering as much of the base as you can. Using your fingertips, press all over the dough to form deep indentations. Sprinkle with the tomatoes, oregano, coarse salt and pepper to taste. Drizzle with the remaining 2 tablespoons (30 mL) oil. Cover with a damp tea towel and let rise an additional 30 minutes.

6. Bake for 30 to 35 minutes, until the top is golden brown and crispy. Serve warm or at room temperature.

Zucchini Cheddar Bread

When the garden and farmers' markets begin to flood with summer squash, my mom and I load up on zucchini to fry up batch upon batch of zucchini fritters. They often disappear as quickly as they're made! This bread was inspired by the flavours in our zucchini fritters. Fresh basil, garlic, zucchini and Parmesan cheese—all that summer goodness! The texture of this bread reminds me of a cross between those favourite fritters and a biscuit, making it perfect for breakfast or a light afternoon snack.

1. Preheat the oven to 350°F (180°C). Grease an 8- x 4-inch (1.5 L) loaf pan.

2. In a large mixing bowl whisk together the eggs, milk and oil until the egg yolks have broken up. Stir in the zucchini, basil, parsley, garlic, cheddar and Parmesan. Sift in the flour, baking powder, salt and pepper. Stir until just combined. Do not overmix!

3. Scrape the batter into the prepared loaf pan and bake for 50 to 55 minutes, until the top is golden brown and a toothpick inserted in the centre comes out clean. Transfer to a rack and let cool completely before removing from the pan.

SERVES: *8*

PREP TIME: *15 minutes*

COOK TIME: *50 minutes*

2 large eggs

1 cup (250 mL) whole milk

½ cup (125 mL) extra-virgin olive oil

1 cup (250 mL) packed grated zucchini

2 tablespoons (30 mL) finely chopped fresh basil

1 tablespoon (15 mL) finely chopped fresh parsley

1 clove garlic, minced

1 cup (250 mL) freshly grated old white cheddar cheese

½ cup (125 mL) freshly grated Parmesan cheese

3 cups (750 mL) all-purpose flour

1 tablespoon (15 mL) baking powder

1 teaspoon (5 mL) salt

½ teaspoon (2 mL) pepper

Jalapeño Cheddar Cornbread

SERVES: *8 to 10*

PREP TIME: *10 minutes*

COOK TIME: *35 minutes*

2 large eggs

1½ cups (375 mL) buttermilk

½ cup (125 mL) unsalted butter, melted

¼ cup (60 mL) turbinado sugar

1¼ cups (300 mL) all-purpose flour

1 cup (250 mL) whole-grain medium-grind cornmeal

1½ teaspoons (7 mL) baking powder

½ teaspoon (2 mL) baking soda

¾ teaspoon (4 mL) fine salt

½ teaspoon (2 mL) black pepper

2 jalapeño peppers, seeded and minced

1½ cups (375 mL) grated old cheddar cheese, plus more for topping

1 jalapeño pepper, thinly sliced, for topping (optional)

To be honest, I am quite the baby when it comes to spicy food, but I am a huge fan of jalapeños. By removing the seeds from the peppers, you remove the bulk of the heat. What's left is the delicious, distinctive jalapeño flavour, and here that's mixed with sharp cheddar cheese and a hint of sweetness for a summer staple that is a fantastic addition to any outdoor barbecue.

1. Preheat the oven to 350°F (180°C). Grease an 8-inch (20 cm) cast-iron skillet.

2. In a large mixing bowl whisk together the eggs, buttermilk, butter and sugar until frothy. Add the flour, cornmeal, baking powder, baking soda, salt and black pepper. Stir until thick. Fold in the minced jalapeños and cheddar.

3. Scrape the batter into the prepared skillet. Top with the sliced jalapeño and additional cheddar, if desired. Bake for 35 to 40 minutes, until the top bounces back when touched or a toothpick inserted in the centre comes out clean. Let cool slightly before slicing and serving.

No-Knead Olive Rosemary Bread

If you aren't familiar with no-knead bread, you need to stop what you are doing and gather everything you need to make a loaf! It is even easier than it sounds. Instead of kneading and proofing until the perfect dough is achieved, you simply stir the ingredients together before bed, let the yeast do its thing overnight, and bake the dough fresh in the morning. It is important to use a Dutch oven while making this bread; for the first part of the baking the lid is left on to steam the inside of the bread, and then it's removed to crisp up the exterior. To make this bread extra special, I add fresh summer rosemary and Kalamata olives.

1. In a large mixing bowl combine the all-purpose flour, whole wheat flour, fine salt and yeast. Stir until combined. Pour in the warm water and stir until a sticky dough forms. Tightly cover the bowl with plastic wrap and let the dough rest at room temperature until doubled in size, about 12 hours.

2. Once the dough has doubled in size, stir in the garlic, olives and rosemary. Turn the dough out onto a heavily floured surface and knead to work in the fillings.

3. Shape the dough into a round loaf. Brush with the oil and sprinkle with the coarse salt and pepper. Cover with a damp tea towel and let rest for 30 minutes while you preheat the oven.

4. Place a lidded 4-quart (3.8 L) Dutch oven in the oven and preheat the oven to 450°F (230°C).

5. Once the oven is preheated, carefully remove the Dutch oven and quickly flour the inside. Lift the round loaf and drop it inside the pot. Place the lid on the Dutch oven and bake for 25 minutes. Remove the lid and bake for an additional 20 minutes, or until the top is crispy and golden brown. Remove from the pot and let cool slightly before slicing.

SERVES: *8 to 10*

PREP TIME: *12 hours*

COOK TIME: *45 minutes*

3½ cups (875 mL) all-purpose flour

1 cup (250 mL) whole wheat flour

2 teaspoons (10 mL) fine salt

1¼ teaspoons (6 mL) instant yeast

2½ cups (625 mL) warm water

1 clove garlic, grated

1½ cups (375 mL) Kalamata olives, pitted and roughly chopped

2 tablespoons (30 mL) roughly chopped fresh rosemary

2 tablespoons (30 mL) extra-virgin olive oil

1 teaspoon (5 mL) coarse salt

¼ teaspoon (1 mL) pepper

Pesto Twist Bread

In the summer, when herbs are growing wild in the garden, my mom and I like to make a large batch of basil pesto. (The store-bought variety, which uses regular oil instead of extra-virgin olive oil, cannot compete!) There's so much you can do with fresh pesto—it can be enjoyed spread on bread or tossed with spaghetti—but I wanted to do something a bit different. Cue: pesto twist bread. Inspired by a babka-style bread, twisted with layers and layers of garden-fresh pesto, this is perfect for making sandwiches, dipping in balsamic vinegar and oil, or simply enjoying as is.

SERVES: *12*

PREP TIME: *2 hours*

COOK TIME: *50 minutes*

1 cup (250 mL) warm water

1 tablespoon (15 mL) active dry yeast

4 tablespoons (60 mL) butter, melted

1 tablespoon (15 mL) raw honey

1 teaspoon (5 mL) fine salt

3 cups (750 mL) all-purpose flour

¾ cup (175 mL) basil pesto, homemade or store-bought

1 cup (250 mL) freshly grated Parmesan cheese

1. To the bowl of a stand mixer add the warm water and sprinkle the yeast over top. Let stand for 5 minutes to allow the yeast to activate. If bubbles do not form on the top, start over with fresh yeast.

2. Add the butter, honey and salt. Fit the mixer with the dough hook. With the mixer on low speed, add the flour 1 cup (250 mL) at a time, mixing until the dough comes together. Knead on medium speed for 5 to 7 minutes, until the dough is smooth and elastic. Cover the bowl with a damp tea towel and let rest at room temperature until doubled in size, about 1 hour.

3. Preheat the oven to 375°F (190°C). Grease a 9- x 5-inch (2 L) loaf pan.

4. On a lightly floured surface, roll out the dough into a 12- x 16-inch (30 x 40 cm) rectangle. Spread the pesto over the entire surface of the dough. Evenly sprinkle with the Parmesan.

5. Starting at the long side, tightly roll up the dough, pinching the seam to seal. Using a sharp knife, slice the dough lengthwise down the centre, cutting all the way through, and turn the halves to expose the inside layers. Twist together the two pieces of dough tightly. Fold the twisted dough in half and twist together tightly a second time. Tuck under the two ends and place in the prepared pan.

6. Bake for 50 to 60 minutes, until the bread is cooked through and the top is golden brown. Transfer to a rack and let cool to room temperature before removing from pan.

Stone Fruit and Prosciutto Pizza

SERVES: *4 to 6*

PREP TIME: *2 hours*

COOK TIME: *20 minutes*

PIZZA DOUGH

1 cup (250 mL) warm water

¾ teaspoon (4 mL) instant yeast

1 tablespoon (15 mL) extra-virgin olive oil

½ teaspoon (2 mL) fine salt

2½ cups (625 mL) all-purpose flour

PIZZA TOPPINGS

2 peaches or nectarines, pitted and sliced

¼ cup (60 mL) extra-virgin olive oil

Salt and pepper

2 cups (500 mL) freshly grated mozzarella cheese

½ cup (125 mL) crumbled Gorgonzola cheese

4 ounces (115 g) thinly sliced prosciutto

½ cup (125 mL) arugula, for garnish

This pizza can be made both in the oven or, if you are feeling a little extra adventurous, on the grill. I love the way the barbecue bubbles the pizza dough and adds a slight charred flavour I crave all winter long. The saltiness from the prosciutto pairs perfectly with the sweet stone fruit. As an Italian, I grew up eating prosciutto-wrapped melon. This pizza is a little spin on that.

1. To the bowl of a stand mixer add the warm water and sprinkle the yeast over top. Let stand for 5 minutes to allow the yeast to activate. If bubbles do not form on the top, start over with fresh yeast.

2. Add the oil and salt. Fit the mixer with the dough hook. With the mixer on low speed, add the flour ½ cup (125 mL) at a time, mixing until the dough comes together. Knead on high speed for 5 to 8 minutes, until the dough is smooth.

3. On a lightly floured surface, shape the dough into a ball. Place back in the mixer bowl, cover with a damp tea towel and let rest at room temperature until doubled in size, about 1 hour.

4. While the dough rests, preheat the barbecue on high heat. Grill the fruit slices for a minute on each side. (This can also be done in a buttered grill pan over medium heat.) Set aside until you are ready to assemble the pizza.

5. Preheat the oven to 425°F (220°C), with a pizza stone if using.

6. Once the dough has risen, turn it out onto a lightly floured surface. Roll it out until ¼ inch (5 mm) thick.

To grill: Brush each side of the dough with oil and season with salt and pepper. Grill for 60 seconds on each side. Transfer to a baking sheet.

To bake: Place the dough directly on a floured baking sheet or the hot pizza stone. Bake for 5 minutes.

7. Sprinkle the partially cooked crust with the mozzarella, Gorgonzola and grilled fruit. Bake for an additional 12 to 15 minutes, until the crust is golden brown and the cheese is bubbling. Top with prosciutto and garnish with arugula.

Fall

I WAIT ALL YEAR for October to come, as it marks the beginning of the most magical three months of the year. I love watching the leaves change colour and drinking gallons of apple cider. Justin and I love spending time outdoors in the fall. We visit the pumpkin patch and bring home pumpkins not only for carving and decorating but for making fresh pumpkin purée. It takes a bit more time, but I find nothing can compete with the flavour of the homemade variety. Whether canned or made from scratch, though, it will come in handy for some of my favourite seasonal baked goods, like my Pumpkin Chocolate Cake (page 129), Maple Pumpkin Pie (page 136) and Glazed Pumpkin Scones (page 147). We're also lucky to live a few houses away from one of the many apple orchards in town. Nothing says fall like freshly picked apples! We buy bushels every year, which I bake with throughout the season. One of my favourite fall recipes is the Almond Apple Rose Tart (page 141). It incorporates the unexpected flavour of almond with fresh apples and is presented in the most beautiful rose shape. There's nothing better than the aroma of cinnamon wafting from the kitchen in the fall, and those warm spices pair beautifully with apples, like in my Pear and Apple Crisp (page 139).

In this chapter you'll also find Thanksgiving-inspired dishes, many of which I cook up every year to serve my family, like my Sourdough, Chorizo and Wild Mushroom Stuffing (page 168). And if you need a new way to use Thanksgiving leftovers, I highly recommend the Turkey Cider Hot Dish (page 175).

Pumpkin Pie Granola

Pumpkin pie for breakfast? Not exactly. But the aroma of this morning staple is perfect for autumn. The second September hits, I dive head first into everything pumpkin spice! This granola is healthy, crunchy and packed with fall flavours. I love white chocolate, and I often incorporate it into my granolas (instead of dark chocolate), as I do here.

1. Preheat the oven to 325°F (160°C). Line a baking sheet with parchment paper.

2. In a large mixing bowl combine the oats, white chocolate, pepitas, pecans, cinnamon, ginger, nutmeg, cloves and salt. Stir until evenly mixed.

3. In a medium mixing bowl combine the sugar, maple syrup, pumpkin purée, olive oil and vanilla. Whisk until smooth. Pour over the oat mixture and toss until the granola is well coated.

4. Spread the granola on the prepared baking sheet. Bake for 45 to 60 minutes, stirring every 15 minutes, until golden brown and toasted. Let cool to room temperature on the baking sheet before transferring to an airtight container. Store at room temperature for up to 2 weeks.

MAKES: *8 cups (2 L)*

PREP TIME: *15 minutes*

COOK TIME: *45 minutes*

3 cups (750 mL) old-fashioned rolled oats

1 cup (250 mL) roughly chopped quality white chocolate

1 cup (250 mL) hulled raw pepitas

1 cup (250 mL) roughly chopped pecans

1 teaspoon (5 mL) cinnamon

1 teaspoon (5 mL) ground ginger

¼ teaspoon (1 mL) nutmeg

¼ teaspoon (1 mL) ground cloves

¼ teaspoon (1 mL) fine salt

⅓ cup (75 mL) packed brown sugar

⅓ cup (75 mL) pure maple syrup

⅓ cup (75 mL) pumpkin purée, homemade or canned

⅓ cup (75 mL) extra-virgin olive oil

1 teaspoon (5 mL) pure vanilla extract

Harvest Breakfast Cookies

MAKES: *12 large cookies*

PREP TIME: *15 minutes*

COOK TIME: *10 minutes*

1¼ cups (300 mL) all-purpose flour

1 cup (250 mL) old-fashioned rolled oats

½ cup (125 mL) turbinado sugar

½ teaspoon (2 mL) baking soda

¼ teaspoon (1 mL) fine salt

½ teaspoon (2 mL) cinnamon

¼ teaspoon (1 mL) nutmeg

1 large egg

¾ cup (175 mL) unsalted butter, melted

½ cup (125 mL) pure maple syrup

1 teaspoon (5 mL) pure vanilla extract

½ cup (125 mL) slivered almonds

½ cup (125 mL) roughly chopped dark chocolate

½ cup (125 mL) dried cranberries

½ cup (125 mL) unsweetened shredded coconut

Yes, there is such a thing as a cookie for breakfast! Actually, if you want to eat a chocolate chip cookie for breakfast, I won't stop you from doing that either. However, this cookie is packed with wholesome ingredients like oats, cranberries, coconut, nuts and pure maple syrup, along with cozy warm spices like cinnamon and nutmeg. It's almost like portable granola, but a little more decadent.

1. In a large mixing bowl combine the flour, oats, sugar, baking soda, salt, cinnamon and nutmeg. Stir until well blended.

2. In a small bowl whisk together the egg, melted butter, maple syrup and vanilla. Pour over the dry ingredients and stir with a wooden spoon until the dough comes together. Fold in the almonds, chocolate, cranberries and coconut. Cover the bowl with plastic wrap and refrigerate for 30 minutes.

3. Preheat the oven to 375°F (190°C). Line a baking sheet with parchment paper.

4. Using a standard ice cream scoop, scoop the dough into 12 large rounds on the prepared baking sheet 2 inches (5 cm) apart. Flatten the dough slightly. Bake for 10 to 12 minutes, until the edges are golden brown. Transfer to racks and let cool completely. Store in an airtight container at room temperature for up to 2 days or in the freezer for up to 2 weeks.

London Fog Cupcakes

I am an avid tea drinker. There is something so relaxing about slowing down to enjoy a freshly steeped cup of tea, sitting on the front porch, watching the leaves change colour. I wanted to incorporate this moment into various desserts, and so this London Fog cupcake was created. Earl Grey's distinctive bergamot flavour makes it a perfect tea to bake with.

1. Preheat the oven to 325°F (160°C). Line a cupcake tin with 12 cupcake liners.

2. To make the London Fog Cupcakes, in a saucepan over low heat, heat the milk and tea. Gently simmer (do not bring to a boil) for 2 minutes. Remove from the heat and let steep for 10 minutes before straining.

3. In the bowl of a stand mixer fitted with the paddle attachment, cream the butter with the sugar until fluffy, about 2 minutes. Add the eggs one at a time, beating well after each addition. Beat in the vanilla. Sift in the flour, baking powder and salt. Mix on low speed until just combined. Slowly pour in the infused milk and beat just until the batter is smooth.

4. Divide the batter evenly among the cupcake liners. Bake for 20 minutes, or until the cupcakes bounce back when touched or a toothpick inserted in the centre comes out clean. Transfer to a rack and let cool in the tin while you prepare the frosting.

5. To make the Whipped Vanilla Buttercream, in the bowl of a stand mixer fitted with the paddle attachment, briefly beat the butter. With the mixer on low speed, beat in the icing sugar 1 cup (250 mL) at a time. Once the sugar is incorporated, turn the mixer to high and beat until the frosting is light and fluffy, about 10 minutes. Add the cream and vanilla and beat until the cream is fully incorporated, about 60 seconds.

6. Transfer the buttercream to a large pastry bag fitted with a large open star tip. Holding the bag vertically above a cupcake, squeeze while moving in a circular motion starting from the outside. Once you reach the centre, stop squeezing and gently lift off. Repeat with the remaining cupcakes.

MAKES: *12 cupcakes*

PREP TIME: *15 minutes*

COOK TIME: *20 minutes*

LONDON FOG CUPCAKES

1 cup (250 mL) whole milk

2 tablespoons (30 mL) loose Earl Grey tea

1 cup (250 mL) unsalted butter, room temperature

1½ cups (375 mL) packed light brown sugar

2 large eggs

1 teaspoon (5 mL) pure vanilla extract

2½ cups (625 mL) all-purpose flour

2 teaspoons (10 mL) baking powder

1 teaspoon (5 mL) fine salt

WHIPPED VANILLA BUTTERCREAM

2 cups (500 mL) unsalted butter, room temperature

4 cups (1 L) icing sugar

⅓ cup (75 mL) heavy cream

1 teaspoon (5 mL) pure vanilla extract

Pumpkin Chocolate Cake

This cake is ridiculously good. It is so moist and flavourful thanks to the pumpkin purée and pumpkin spices. I decided to frost it as a naked cake because I wanted the two-tone cake layers to show through. The colours just look so . . . fall, I can't get enough! It is not often you find pumpkin paired with chocolate, but one bite of this cake will convince you it is the perfect combination.

1. Preheat the oven to 350°F (180°C). Grease four 8-inch (20 cm) round cake pans.

2. To make the Pumpkin Cake, in a large mixing bowl combine the eggs, sugar, pumpkin purée, milk, oil and vanilla. Whisk until smooth.

3. In a medium mixing bowl sift the flour, baking soda, baking powder, salt, ginger, cinnamon and nutmeg. Gradually add the flour mixture into the wet ingredients, whisking until the batter is silky smooth. Evenly divide batter between 2 of the prepared cake pans and smooth the tops. Bake for 20 to 25 minutes, until the cakes bounce back when touched or a toothpick inserted in the centre comes out clean. Transfer to racks and let the cakes cool in their pans for 20 minutes before turning out onto racks to cool completely.

4. While the Pumpkin Cake is baking, make the Pumpkin Chocolate Cake. In a large mixing bowl combine the eggs, sugar, pumpkin purée, milk, oil and vanilla. Whisk until smooth.

5. In a medium mixing bowl sift the flour, cocoa powder, baking soda, baking powder, salt, ginger, cinnamon and nutmeg. Gradually add the flour mixture into the wet ingredients, whisking until the batter is silky smooth. Evenly divide between the remaining 2 prepared cake pans and smooth the tops. Bake for 25 to 30 minutes, until the cakes bounce back when touched or a toothpick inserted in the centre comes out clean. Transfer to racks and let the cakes cool in their pans for 20 minutes before turning out onto racks to cool completely.

Continues

SERVES: *12 to 14*

PREP TIME: *60 minutes*

COOK TIME: *20 minutes*

PUMPKIN CAKE

2 large eggs

1½ cups (375 mL) turbinado sugar

1 cup (250 mL) pumpkin purée, homemade or canned

½ cup (125 mL) whole milk

½ cup (125 mL) canola oil

1 teaspoon (5 mL) pure vanilla extract

1¾ cups (425 mL) all-purpose flour

1 teaspoon (5 mL) baking soda

½ teaspoon (2 mL) baking powder

½ teaspoon (2 mL) fine salt

1 teaspoon (5 mL) ground ginger

1 teaspoon (5 mL) cinnamon

½ teaspoon (2 mL) nutmeg

PUMPKIN CHOCOLATE CAKE

2 large eggs

1½ cups (375 mL) turbinado sugar

1 cup (250 mL) pumpkin purée, homemade or canned

½ cup (125 mL) whole milk

½ cup (125 mL) canola oil

1 teaspoon (5 mL) pure vanilla extract

1½ cups (375 mL) all-purpose flour

⅓ cup (75 mL) Dutch-processed cocoa powder

1 teaspoon (5 mL) baking soda

½ teaspoon (2 mL) baking powder

½ teaspoon (2 mL) fine salt

1 teaspoon (5 mL) ground ginger

1 teaspoon (5 mL) cinnamon

½ teaspoon (2 mL) nutmeg

CREAM CHEESE FROSTING

¾ cup (175 mL) unsalted butter,
room temperature

3 cups (750 mL) icing sugar

1 teaspoon (5 mL) pure vanilla
extract

8 ounces (225 g) full-fat cream
cheese, cold

¼ cup (60 mL) hulled raw
pepitas, for serving (optional)

6. While the cakes cool, make the Cream Cheese Frosting. In the bowl of a stand mixer fitted with the paddle attachment, cream the butter, icing sugar and vanilla until fluffy. Turn the mixer to low speed and add the cream cheese 1 ounce (28 g) at a time. Once all of the cream cheese has been added, beat on high speed for an additional 30 seconds.

7. Once the cakes have cooled, use a serrated knife to level each cake, removing any domed top that may have formed.

8. Place a layer of the chocolate pumpkin cake, cut side up, on a cake stand or cake turntable. Spoon approximately ¾ cup (175 mL) frosting onto the middle. Using an offset spatula, smooth the frosting flat, spreading it to the edges. Place a layer of the pumpkin cake, cut side up, on top and gently press down to stabilize it. Spread another ¾ cup (175 mL) frosting over the top and smooth flat. Repeat with the second layers of the chocolate pumpkin cake and pumpkin cake, placing the final layer cut side down. Gently press down the top layer to stabilize and level the cake. Dollop the remaining frosting onto the top and use the offset spatula to gently work the frosting evenly over the top and down the sides. Be sure to coat every inch of the cake with frosting.

9. For a "naked" finish, hold the edge of an offset spatula or bench scraper against the cake and slowly turn the cake, scraping away the frosting to expose the layers of cake. Wipe the edge of the spatula clean of frosting as you go. This will result in a beautiful naked cake. Sprinkle the top with the pepitas, if desired. Serve the cake immediately or store in the fridge, covered, for up to 24 hours before serving.

Apple Cheddar Pie

A classic apple pie was the first pie I ever mastered. Once I perfected the basic recipe, I decided it was time to experiment with different flavour combinations. One day I was feeling adventurous, so I incorporated cheddar. It might sound strange, but give it a try! The cheddar offers just a hint of sharpness to offset the sweetness of the apples. Once you've tried this combination, you'll find yourself reaching for cheddar every time you make an apple pie.

SERVES: *6 to 8*

PREP TIME: *20 minutes*

COOK TIME: *50 minutes*

CHEDDAR PIE DOUGH

3 cups (750 mL) all-purpose flour, sifted

½ teaspoon (2 mL) fine salt

¾ cup (175 mL) unsalted butter, cold and cubed

⅓ cup (75 mL) shortening, cold

1½ cups (375 mL) finely grated aged cheddar cheese, divided

½ cup (125 mL) ice water

1 egg, whisked, for egg wash

APPLE PIE FILLING

6 cups (1.5 L) peeled, cored and thinly sliced apples

¾ cup (175 mL) turbinado sugar

1 tablespoon (15 mL) cornstarch

¼ teaspoon (1 mL) nutmeg

1 teaspoon (5 mL) pure vanilla extract

1 tablespoon (15 mL) fresh lemon juice

1. To make the Cheddar Pie Dough, in a large mixing bowl sift together the flour and salt. Add the butter and shortening. Using your hands or a pastry cutter, work in the butter and shortening until the mixture forms pea-sized crumbs. Stir in 1 cup (250 mL) of the cheddar. Incorporate the ice water 1 tablespoon (15 mL) at a time until the dough begins to come together.

2. Turn the dough out onto a lightly floured surface, divide it into two equal portions, and shape each into a disc. Wrap in plastic wrap and refrigerate for 2 hours or until ready to use. (The dough can be made a day or two in advance.)

3. Preheat the oven to 375°F (190°C).

4. To make the Apple Pie Filling, in a large mixing bowl combine the apples, sugar, cornstarch, nutmeg, vanilla and lemon juice. Toss to coat. Set aside while you roll out the pie dough.

5. On a lightly floured surface, roll out one disc of dough until ⅛ inch (3 mm) thick. Gently lift and transfer the dough to a 9-inch (23 cm) pie plate, pressing the dough into the bottom and sides of the plate. Trim the dough edges, leaving a ½-inch (1 cm) overhang. Fold under the overhang, then crimp the edges. To crimp the edges, place an index finger on the lip of the pie plate and pinch around that finger with the index finger and thumb of your other hand, holding the dough in between. Scrape the Apple Pie Filling into the pie shell and arrange the apple slices so they lie flat.

Continues

6. Roll out the remaining dough until ⅛ inch (3 mm) thick. Using a small leaf-shaped pastry cutter, cut the dough into approximately 75 leaves. Line the outside edge of the crust with slightly overlapping leaves. Continue layering the leaves, working your way to the centre, making sure to not leave any gaps but leaving a small hole in the very centre for steam to escape. Brush the top of the pie with the egg wash and top with the remaining ½ cup (125 mL) cheddar.

7. Bake for 50 to 60 minutes, until the top is golden brown. Let cool completely before serving.

Salted Caramel Pear Hand Pies

Salted caramel is one of my favourite sauces. I always make an extra-big batch so I have a jar ready to go in the fridge when I need it (or when I just want a spoonful—you never know when a salted caramel craving will strike!). I prefer to use Anjou pears here: they hold their shape nicely in tarts and pies and don't become mushy.

1. Preheat the oven to 375°F (190°C). Line a baking sheet with parchment paper.

2. In a medium saucepan combine the butter, pears, sugar, lemon juice, vanilla, nutmeg and salt. Stir over medium heat until the pears soften, about 10 minutes. Remove from the heat.

3. On a lightly floured surface, roll out the chilled pie dough to a 16- x 18-inch (40 x 46 cm) rectangle. The pastry should be ¼ inch (5 mm) thick. Cut into twenty-four 2- x 3-inch (5 x 8 cm) rectangles.

4. Place a tablespoon (15 mL) of filling in the centre of 12 of the pastry rectangles and drizzle each lightly with 2 teaspoons (10 mL) Salted Caramel Sauce. Lightly brush the edges with egg wash. Place a second pastry rectangle on top of each, and press down the edges with a fork to seal. Transfer the hand pies to the prepared baking sheet and brush the tops with the egg wash.

5. Bake for 20 minutes, or until the pastry is golden brown. Remove from the oven and drizzle with additional Salted Caramel Sauce, if desired. Serve warm or at room temperature. Store in an airtight container at room temperature for up to 2 days or in the freezer for up to 2 weeks.

MAKES: *12 hand pies*

PREP TIME: *15 minutes*

COOK TIME: *20 minutes*

2 tablespoons (30 mL) unsalted butter, room temperature

3 medium Anjou pears, peeled, cored and diced

½ cup (125 mL) turbinado sugar

1 tablespoon (15 mL) fresh lemon juice

1 teaspoon (5 mL) pure vanilla extract

¼ teaspoon (1 mL) nutmeg

¼ teaspoon (1 mL) fine salt

1 batch Hand Pie Pastry (page 91), chilled

1 batch Salted Caramel Sauce (page 241), plus more for drizzling (optional)

1 egg, whisked, for egg wash

Maple Pumpkin Pie

SERVES: *6 to 8*

PREP TIME: *4 hours*

COOK TIME: *45 minutes*

MAPLE PUMPKIN PIE

1 batch Single Pie Dough (page 243), chilled

4 large eggs

2½ cups (625 mL) pumpkin purée, homemade or canned

1½ cups (375 mL) heavy cream

¾ cup (175 mL) turbinado sugar

½ cup (125 mL) pure maple syrup

1 tablespoon (15 mL) pure vanilla extract

1 teaspoon (5 mL) ground ginger

1 teaspoon (5 mL) cinnamon

½ teaspoon (2 mL) nutmeg

½ teaspoon (2 mL) fine salt

MAPLE WHIPPED CREAM

1 cup (250 mL) heavy cream

1 tablespoon (15 mL) pure maple syrup

1 teaspoon (5 mL) pure vanilla extract

Pinch of cinnamon

It's not officially fall until you've taken a bite of pumpkin pie. This one has a Canadian twist with the addition of maple syrup. Maple and pumpkin pair perfectly together, and I love using a more natural sweetener when baking. Even the whipped cream is sweetened with maple syrup to make it a little extra special. After all, you can't have pumpkin pie without whipped cream!

1. Preheat the oven to 375°F (190°C).

2. On a lightly floured surface, roll out the pie dough until ⅛ inch (3 mm) thick. Gently lift and transfer the dough to a 9-inch (23 cm) pie plate, pressing the dough into the bottom and sides of the plate. Trim the dough edges, leaving a 1-inch (2.5 cm) overhang. Fold under the overhang, then crimp the edges. To crimp the edges, place an index finger on the lip of the pie plate and pinch around that finger with the index finger and thumb of your other hand, holding the dough in between. Refrigerate while you prepare the filling.

3. In a large mixing bowl beat the eggs. Add the pumpkin purée, cream, sugar, maple syrup, vanilla, ginger, cinnamon, nutmeg and salt. Whisk until the filling is silky smooth.

4. Pour the filling into the prepared pie shell. Bake for 45 to 55 minutes, until the crust is golden brown and the filling still has a slight jiggle in the centre. Transfer to a rack and let set at room temperature for 4 to 6 hours.

5. Prepare the Maple Whipped Cream. Whisk together the cream, maple syrup, vanilla and cinnamon until stiff peaks form. Refrigerate until ready to serve. (This can be made up to 24 hours in advance.)

Pear and Apple Crisp

When we think of fall desserts, typically apples and pumpkins spring to mind. But what about pears! With a similar texture to apples, but a different and distinctive taste, these two work really well mixed together. This crisp combines the best of both worlds. Since pears and apples both come into season in the late summer, they are the perfect way to kick off fall!

1. Preheat the oven to 350°F (180°C).

2. In a large mixing bowl combine the apples, pears, sugar, cornstarch, cinnamon, nutmeg and vanilla. Toss to coat. Transfer the filling to a 9- x 12-inch (3 L) baking dish and set aside while you prepare the topping.

3. In a medium mixing bowl combine the oats, flour, sugar, pecans, salt and nutmeg. Stir until evenly mixed. Add the butter. Using your hands, work the butter into the oat mixture until a crumbly mixture is formed. Evenly disperse the topping over the fruit.

4. Bake for 45 to 50 minutes, until the top is golden brown and the fruit filling is bubbling. Serve warm or at room temperature with vanilla ice cream.

SERVES: *6 to 8*

PREP TIME: *20 minutes*

COOK TIME: *45 minutes*

PEAR APPLE FILLING

5 medium apples, peeled, cored and sliced

5 medium pears, peeled, cored and sliced

¾ cup (175 mL) turbinado sugar

2 tablespoons (30 mL) cornstarch

1 teaspoon (5 mL) cinnamon

¼ teaspoon (1 mL) nutmeg

1 teaspoon (5 mL) pure vanilla extract

CRISP TOPPING

1 cup (250 mL) old-fashioned rolled oats

1 cup (250 mL) all-purpose flour

¾ cup (175 mL) turbinado sugar

½ cup (125 mL) pecans, roughly chopped

½ teaspoon (2 mL) fine salt

Pinch of nutmeg

½ cup (125 mL) unsalted butter, cold and cubed

FOR SERVING

Vanilla ice cream

Almond Apple Rose Tart

This tart is elegant and gorgeous, and most important, simple to make. For the longest time, I avoided baking apple rose tarts because it looked like so much precision was involved and I assumed they required a fancy kitchen tool to slice the apples. None of that is true! I just thinly slice the apples crosswise and cook them briefly so they're more flexible to work with. The almond filling reminds me of a less sweet version of marzipan. This might be one of my favourite desserts in the book!

1. To make the Almond Tart Crust, in a large mixing bowl stir together the flour, almond meal, sugar and salt. Add the cubed butter and work it in with your hands until the mixture forms pea-sized crumbs.

2. In a small bowl whisk together the egg yolk, water and vanilla. Pour over the crumb mixture and work it in with your hands just until the dough begins to hold together.

3. Transfer the dough to an 8-inch (20 cm) tart pan with a removable bottom and press over the bottom and up the sides to form an even ¼-inch (5 mm) thick crust. Place the tart shell in the refrigerator while you prepare the remaining layers.

4. Preheat the oven to 350°F (180°C).

5. To make the Almond Tart Filling, in a medium mixing bowl combine the sugar, butter, eggs, vanilla and almond extract. Whisk until blended. Using a wooden spoon, stir in the almond meal, flour and salt until smooth. Set aside.

6. To make the Apple Rose, in a large saucepan combine the apples, cider and sugar. Toss to coat. Cover and cook over medium heat for 2 to 3 minutes, until the apples have slightly softened but still hold their shape. Remove from the heat, uncover and let stand until cool enough to handle.

Continues

SERVES: *6 to 8*

PREP TIME: *20 minutes*

COOK TIME: *30 minutes*

ALMOND TART CRUST

1 cup (250 mL) all-purpose flour

½ cup (125 mL) almond meal

¼ cup (60 mL) turbinado sugar

¼ teaspoon (1 mL) fine salt

6 tablespoons (90 mL) unsalted butter, cold and cubed

1 large egg yolk

2 tablespoons (30 mL) ice water

1 teaspoon (5 mL) pure vanilla extract

ALMOND TART FILLING

½ cup (125 mL) turbinado sugar

6 tablespoons (90 mL) unsalted butter, melted

2 large eggs

1 teaspoon (5 mL) pure vanilla extract

1 teaspoon (5 mL) pure almond extract

½ cup (125 mL) almond meal

½ cup (125 mL) all-purpose flour

¼ teaspoon (1 mL) fine salt

APPLE ROSE

5 medium apples, cored, thinly sliced crosswise and cut into half-moons

¼ cup (60 mL) sweet apple cider

2 tablespoons (30 mL) turbinado sugar

7. To assemble the tart, pour the Almond Tart Filling into the tart shell and smooth flat with an offset spatula. Beginning at the outside edge of the tart, arrange the half-moon apple slices, skin side up and slightly overlapping, in a circle. Continue to make a spiral, working your way to the centre of the tart, keeping the apple slices close together and tight.

8. Bake for 25 to 30 minutes, until the crust and apple slices are golden. Let cool to room temperature before serving, about 30 minutes.

BAKER'S NOTE In this recipe almond meal and almond flour can be used interchangeably. Use a firm flesh apple that will hold its shape, such as Honeycrisp, Northern Spy or Golden Delicious.

Pecan Sticky Buns

A Sunday morning isn't complete without a freshly baked batch of sticky buns. I am a huge lover of cinnamon rolls, but sticky buns take things to a whole new level. Topped with a mound of gooey, sweet caramel sauce and crunchy pecans? Yes, please! This recipe is a classic, and you'll find yourself wanting to make these every chance you get. For those of you who are team cinnamon roll, these buns just might make you change your mind.

1. To make the Sticky Bun Dough, to the bowl of a stand mixer add the warm water and sprinkle the yeast over top. Let stand for 5 minutes to allow the yeast to activate. If bubbles do not form on the top, start over with fresh yeast.

2. Whisk in the egg, milk, butter, vanilla, sugar and salt. Fit the mixer with the dough hook. With the mixer on low speed, add the flour 1 cup (250 mL) at a time, mixing until the dough comes together. Knead on medium speed for 8 to 10 minutes, until the dough is smooth and elastic.

3. On a lightly floured surface, shape the dough into a ball. Place it back in the mixer bowl, cover with a damp tea towel and let rest at room temperature until doubled in size, about 2 hours.

4. Preheat the oven to 375°F (190°C).

5. Once the dough has risen, on a lightly floured surface roll it out to a 15- x 9-inch (38 x 23 cm) rectangle.

6. For the Sticky Bun Filling, in a small bowl stir together the brown sugar and cinnamon. Brush the dough with the melted butter, leaving a 1-inch (2.5 cm) border, and sprinkle with the cinnamon sugar. Beginning at a long side, carefully roll into a tight log, pinching the seam to seal. Slice into 1½-inch (4 cm) rounds. Discard the end pieces.

Continues

SERVES: *8*

PREP TIME: *2 hours*

COOK TIME: *40 minutes*

STICKY BUN DOUGH

¼ cup (60 mL) warm water

1 package (¼ ounce/8g) instant yeast

1 large egg

1 cup (250 mL) whole milk

⅓ cup (75 mL) unsalted butter, melted

1 teaspoon (5 mL) pure vanilla extract

⅓ cup (75 mL) granulated sugar

½ teaspoon (2 mL) fine salt

4 cups (1 L) all-purpose flour

STICKY BUN FILLING

¾ cup (175 mL) packed light brown sugar

1 tablespoon (15 mL) cinnamon

4 tablespoons (60 mL) unsalted butter, melted

CARAMEL SAUCE

½ cup (125 mL) unsalted butter

1 cup (250 mL) packed light brown sugar

¼ cup (60 mL) pure maple syrup

1 teaspoon (5 mL) pure vanilla extract

½ cup (125 mL) pecans, roughly chopped

7. For the Caramel Sauce, melt the butter in a small saucepan over low heat. Add the brown sugar, maple syrup and vanilla. Stir until the sugar has fully dissolved. Pour the sauce into a 10-inch (2.5 L) round baking dish. Evenly sprinkle the pecans over top. Top with the sliced dough rounds, cut side down. Let rise covered for 15 minutes.

8. Bake for 30 to 35 minutes, until the rolls are golden brown and cooked through. Let cool in the pan to room temperature before flipping onto a platter and removing the pan.

Glazed Pumpkin Scones

When fall rolls around, I am that person who indulges in everything pumpkin spice. (I would put pumpkin spice into every dessert if I could!) These scones are packed with fall flavour and are probably my favourite scones to date. The pumpkin purée gives them the perfect orange hue and helps keep them extra moist.

1. Preheat the oven to 375°F (190°C). Line a baking sheet with parchment paper.

2. To make the Pumpkin Scones, in a large mixing bowl combine the flour, sugar, baking powder, baking soda, salt, cinnamon, ginger, nutmeg and cloves. Stir until well blended. Add the cubed butter. Using your hands or a pastry cutter, work in the butter until the mixture resembles pea-sized crumbs.

3. In a medium mixing bowl whisk together the egg, pumpkin purée, milk and vanilla. Pour over the dry ingredients and stir until the dough comes together.

4. Turn the dough out onto a lightly floured surface and shape into a disc 1 inch (2.5 cm) thick. Cut into 8 even wedges. Arrange the wedges on the prepared baking sheet.

5. Bake for 15 minutes, until the scones are golden brown on top. Let cool for 15 minutes on a rack before glazing.

6. While the scones are cooling, make the Vanilla Glaze. In a small bowl combine the icing sugar, vanilla and milk. Stir until smooth. The glaze should coat the back of a spoon. If it is runny, stir in a touch more icing sugar. If it is too thick to be spreadable, stir in a touch more milk. Once the scones have cooled slightly, brush their tops with the glaze.

7. Lastly, make the Pumpkin Glaze. In a small bowl combine the icing sugar, milk, pumpkin purée, cinnamon, ginger, nutmeg, and cloves. Stir until the same consistency as the Vanilla Glaze. Using a spoon or fork, drizzle a touch of glaze over each scone. Store in an airtight container for up to 48 hours.

MAKES: *8 scones*

PREP TIME: *20 minutes*

COOK TIME: *15 minutes*

PUMPKIN SCONES

2 cups (500 mL) all-purpose flour

¾ cup (175 mL) packed light brown sugar

2 teaspoons (10 mL) baking powder

½ teaspoon (2 mL) baking soda

½ teaspoon (2 mL) fine salt

1 teaspoon (5 mL) cinnamon

1 teaspoon (5 mL) ground ginger

¼ teaspoon (1 mL) nutmeg

¼ teaspoon (1 mL) ground cloves

½ cup (125 mL) unsalted butter, cold and cubed

1 large egg

½ cup (125 mL) pumpkin purée, homemade or canned

⅓ cup (75 mL) whole milk

1 teaspoon (5 mL) pure vanilla extract

VANILLA GLAZE

1 cup (250 mL) icing sugar

2 teaspoons (10 mL) pure vanilla extract

1 teaspoon (5 mL) whole milk

PUMPKIN GLAZE

½ cup (125 mL) icing sugar

1 teaspoon (5 mL) whole milk

½ teaspoon (2 mL) pumpkin purée, homemade or canned

Pinch of cinnamon

Pinch of ground ginger

Pinch of nutmeg

Pinch of ground cloves

Ultimate Banana Bread

MAKES: *1 loaf*

PREP TIME: *15 minutes*

COOK TIME: *50 minutes*

3 large very ripe bananas, mashed

4 tablespoons (60 mL) unsalted
butter, melted

¼ cup (60 mL) canola oil

¼ cup (60 mL) plain or vanilla
full-fat yogurt

1 cup (250 mL) + 1 tablespoon
(15 mL) turbinado sugar,
divided

1 large egg

1 teaspoon (5 mL) pure vanilla
extract

1½ cups (375 mL) all-purpose
flour

1 teaspoon (5 mL) cinnamon

1 teaspoon (5 mL) baking soda

¼ teaspoon (1 mL) fine salt

Banana bread is essential in my house—Justin and I make this loaf at least once a week. I just couldn't write a baking book without including a solid recipe for this classic. I experimented with countless versions of banana bread before perfecting this one. I promise, your search for the perfect banana bread ends here. My recipe uses a combination of butter and oil, which helps keep it both flavourful and moist. Be sure to use the ripest bananas for maximum natural sweetness. (I love watching uneaten bananas turn brown on my countertop—I know they mean a fresh loaf of banana bread is in my near future!) If you want to mix things up, add nuts, raisins, peanut butter or chocolate chips. Don't be afraid to get creative!

1. Preheat the oven to 325°F (160°C). Grease an 8- x 4-inch (1.5 L) loaf pan.

2. In a large mixing bowl combine the bananas, butter, oil, yogurt and 1 cup (250 mL) of the sugar. Whisk until well blended. Whisk in the egg and vanilla.

3. In a medium mixing bowl sift the flour, cinnamon, baking soda and salt. Add the dry ingredients to the wet ingredients and stir until just combined. Scrape the batter into the prepared loaf pan and sprinkle with the remaining 1 tablespoon (15 mL) sugar.

4. Bake for 50 minutes, or until the top is golden brown and bounces back when touched or a toothpick inserted in the centre comes out clean. Transfer to a rack and let cool to room temperature before removing from the pan.

Baked Apple Cider Doughnuts

Is it really fall without apple cider doughnuts? Many years ago my family and I went to a small town in upstate New York for Thanksgiving, and that weekend just happened to be their apple festival. Jackpot! We ate every sort of apple treat you can imagine, but I've never forgotten the freshly fried apple cider doughnuts. I've created a simple baked version for this book. Flavoured with the freshest pressed apple cider, each doughnut is brushed with butter and rolled in cinnamon sugar for the perfect finish.

1. Preheat the oven to 375°F (190°C). Grease a 6-mould doughnut pan.

2. In a large mixing bowl combine ½ cup (125 mL) of the melted butter, ½ cup (125 mL) of the granulated sugar, the brown sugar, eggs and vanilla. Beat until fluffy, about 2 minutes. Stir in the apple cider and milk until incorporated.

3. Sift in the flour, baking powder, 1 teaspoon (5 mL) of the cinnamon and salt. Stir until smooth.

4. Spoon the batter into the doughnut pan, filling each mould three-quarters full. Bake for 15 minutes, or until the tops are golden brown and a toothpick inserted in the centre comes out clean. Let cool in the pan for 2 minutes before turning out onto a rack. Repeat to make 6 more doughnuts.

5. In a bowl stir together the remaining 1 cup (250 mL) granulated sugar and the remaining ¼ cup (60 mL) cinnamon.

6. Dip each side of a doughnut in the remaining ½ cup (125 mL) melted butter and roll in the cinnamon sugar. Repeat with the remaining doughnuts. Serve immediately or store in an airtight container at room temperature for up to 2 days or in the freezer for up to 2 weeks.

MAKES: *12 doughnuts*

PREP TIME: *15 minutes*

COOK TIME: *15 minutes*

1 cup (250 mL) unsalted butter, melted, divided

1½ cups (375 mL) granulated sugar, divided

½ cup (125 mL) packed light brown sugar

2 large eggs

1 teaspoon (5 mL) pure vanilla extract

¾ cup (175 mL) sweet apple cider

¼ cup (60 mL) whole milk

2½ cups (625 mL) all-purpose flour

1½ teaspoons (7 mL) baking powder

¼ cup (60 mL) + 1 teaspoon (5 mL) cinnamon, divided

1 teaspoon (5 mL) fine salt

Pumpkin Ginger Waffles

SERVES: *4 to 6*

PREP TIME: *10 minutes*

COOK TIME: *20 minutes*

2 large eggs, separated

1 cup (250 mL) pumpkin purée, homemade or canned

⅓ cup (75 mL) unsalted butter, melted

¼ cup (60 mL) turbinado sugar

¼ cup (60 mL) pure maple syrup, plus more for serving

2 teaspoons (10 mL) grated fresh ginger

1 teaspoon (5 mL) pure vanilla extract

1½ cups (375 mL) all-purpose flour

2 tablespoons (30 mL) cornstarch

1 tablespoon (15 mL) baking powder

¼ teaspoon (1 mL) fine salt

½ teaspoon (2 mL) cinnamon

¼ teaspoon (1 mL) nutmeg

Fresh Whipped Cream (page 240), for serving

These waffles are perfect for a cozy fall weekend. I use grated fresh ginger here for its extra kick of flavour, and it also complements the other warm spices. I like to make a batch of these on Sunday mornings and then toast any leftovers throughout the week. I love enjoying a plate of these waffles, sipping a pumpkin spice latte and watching the crisp leaves fall.

1. In a large mixing bowl whisk the egg yolks. Add the pumpkin purée, butter, sugar, maple syrup, ginger and vanilla. Whisk until smooth. Sift in the flour, cornstarch, baking powder, salt, cinnamon and nutmeg. Stir until just incorporated.

2. In a medium mixing bowl whisk the egg whites to stiff peaks. Gently fold them into the batter, being careful not to deflate the whites.

3. Preheat a waffle iron and spray with nonstick cooking spray. Cook the waffles according to your iron's directions for 3 to 5 minutes, or until the edges are crisp and golden brown.

4. Plate the waffles and top generously with maple syrup and Fresh Whipped Cream. Any leftovers can be individually wrapped in plastic wrap and stored in the freezer for up to 2 weeks.

Sweet Potato Sage Biscuits

A bite out of these fluffy, light biscuits is like a bite of Thanksgiving! Sage always reminds me of the holidays, but the sweet potato takes me right to Thanksgiving. Just a quick tip: be sure your mashed sweet potato is completely cooled, as you don't want to risk melting the butter! The cold butter is what yields the flakiest of biscuits.

1. Preheat the oven to 400°F (200°C). Line a baking sheet with parchment paper.

2. In a large mixing bowl whisk together the flour, sage, sugar, baking powder and salt. Add the butter and work in using your hands or a pastry cutter until the mixture forms pea-sized crumbs. Stir in the sweet potato and milk. If the dough is a little wet, add a touch more flour.

3. Turn the dough out onto a heavily floured surface and pat out until 1 inch (2.5 cm) thick. Using a 2½-inch (6 cm) round biscuit cutter, cut out 8 biscuits. Scraps can be rerolled. Place on the prepared baking sheet.

4. Brush the tops with the egg wash. Bake for 15 to 20 minutes, until the biscuits have puffed and the tops are golden brown. Let cool on a rack for 15 minutes before serving. Store in an airtight container at room temperature for up to 2 days or in the freezer for up to 2 weeks.

BAKER'S NOTE If you don't have a cookie cutter, you can use a mason jar lid or water glass to cut out the biscuit rounds.

MAKES: *8 biscuits*

PREP TIME: *20 minutes*

COOK TIME: *15 minutes*

1½ cups (375 mL) all-purpose flour

2 tablespoons (30 mL) finely chopped fresh sage

1 tablespoon (15 mL) turbinado sugar

1 tablespoon (15 mL) baking powder

1 teaspoon (5 mL) fine salt

½ cup (125 mL) unsalted butter, cold and cubed

1 cup (250 mL) mashed sweet potato, cooled completely

½ cup (125 mL) whole milk

1 egg, whisked, for egg wash

Broccoli Cheddar Pinwheels

MAKES: *8 to 10 rolls*

PREP TIME: *2 hours*

COOK TIME: *20 minutes*

1 batch Pizza Dough (page 118)

¼ cup (60 mL) extra-virgin olive oil

2 cloves garlic, minced

1 tablespoon (15 mL) finely chopped fresh parsley

Salt and pepper

1 cup (250 mL) roughly chopped steamed broccoli

2 cups (500 mL) grated old cheddar cheese

4 ounces (115 g) thinly sliced deli ham

This is a fun back-to-school recipe for the whole family to help make! Pack them for a Friday pizza lunch or have them ready as an after-school snack. These pinwheels are similar to cinnamon rolls, but with a savoury twist: homemade pizza dough filled with broccoli, cheddar cheese and ham. You can honestly add anything you'd like to the mix. I love dipping them in marinara sauce too.

1. Make the Pizza Dough and let it rise until doubled in size, about 1 hour.

2. Preheat the oven to 375°F (190°C). Line a baking sheet with parchment paper.

3. Whisk together the olive oil, garlic, parsley, and salt and pepper to taste. Set aside.

4. Once the dough has risen, roll it out on a lightly floured surface into a 14- x 16-inch (35 x 40 cm) rectangle. Brush the entire surface of the dough with the olive oil mixture. Sprinkle with the broccoli and cheddar. Cover with the sliced ham. Beginning at a long side, carefully roll into a tight log, pinching the seam to seal. Slice into 1-inch (2.5 cm) rounds. Discard the end pieces.

5. Arrange the rounds cut side up on the prepared baking sheet. Bake for 20 minutes, or until golden brown and doubled in size. Let cool for 15 minutes on the baking sheet before serving. Store in an airtight container in the refrigerator for up to 4 days.

BAKER'S NOTE If you don't have time to make your own dough from scratch, you can use a store-bought fresh pizza dough.

Everything Bagel Crackers

Two of my favourite after-school snacks when I was growing up were melted cheddar cheese on crackers and a toasted everything bagel. This recipe combines the best of both worlds: cheddar in the cracker and a generous sprinkle of everything bagel seasoning on top. Kids and adults alike will love these as an afternoon snack.

1. Preheat the oven to 350°F (180°C). Line a baking sheet with parchment paper.

2. To make the Crackers, in a large mixing bowl whisk together the water, butter, honey, salt and garlic. Sift in the flour, then add the cheddar. Stir until the dough comes together.

3. Turn the dough out onto a heavily floured surface and roll out until ¼ inch (5 mm) thick. Using a pastry wheel cut into bite-size squares. Arrange the squares fairly close together on the prepared baking sheet.

4. To make the Everything Bagel Seasoning, in a small bowl toss together the sesame seeds, poppy seeds, onion flakes, garlic flakes and salt. Sprinkle the seasoning over the crackers, gently pressing down into each cracker.

5. Bake for 5 to 7 minutes, until the edges are golden brown. Let cool to room temperature before eating. Store in an airtight container at room temperature for up to a week.

MAKES: *about 50 crackers*

PREP TIME: *15 minutes*

COOK TIME: *5 minutes*

CRACKERS

1 cup (250 mL) water

½ cup (125 mL) butter, melted

2 tablespoons (30 mL) raw honey

2 teaspoons (10 mL) fine salt

1 clove garlic, grated

3 cups (750 mL) all-purpose flour

¾ cup (175 mL) grated cheddar cheese

EVERYTHING BAGEL SEASONING

1 teaspoon (5 mL) sesame seeds

1 teaspoon (5 mL) poppy seeds

1 teaspoon (5 mL) dried onion flakes

1 teaspoon (5 mL) dried garlic flakes

½ teaspoon (2 mL) coarse salt

Asiago Cheddar Pretzels

As the leaves change colours and the weather turns cool, I start making my favourite comfort foods. It didn't take me long to realize that they almost always involve cheese! These pretzels are at the top of my list. I remember the first time Justin and I decided to make pretzels from scratch. We thought it would be so difficult to make the perfect pretzel dough, but it turned out to be as easy as making pizza dough. (Just don't ask us how many pretzels we each ate that night.) These are a great addition to any party spread—especially an Oktoberfest-themed one!

1. To the bowl of a stand mixer add the warm water and sprinkle the yeast over top. Let stand for 5 minutes to allow the yeast to activate. If bubbles do not form on the top, start over with fresh yeast.

2. Whisk in the honey and salt. Fit the mixer with the dough hook. With the mixer on low speed, add 1 cup (250 mL) of the flour, followed by the melted butter, mixing until incorporated. Add the remaining flour 1 cup (250 mL) at a time, mixing until the dough comes together. Knead on medium speed for 5 to 7 minutes, until the dough is smooth and elastic. Using your hands, fold in the cheddar and Asiago.

3. On a lightly floured surface, shape the dough into a ball. Place back in the mixer bowl, cover with a damp tea towel and let rest at room temperature until doubled in size, about 2 hours.

4. Preheat the oven to 425°F (220°C). Line a baking sheet with parchment paper.

5. In a large pot, bring 8 cups (2 L) water to a boil. Whisk in the baking soda.

6. Divide the dough into 12 equal pieces. Using your palms, roll each piece into a rope approximately 15 inches (38 cm) long. Working with one rope at a time, take each end of the rope with your fingers and create a U shape, with the ends pointing away from you. Holding an end in each hand, twist the ropes together once. Still holding the ends, fold the twist towards the bottom of the U shape. Pinch the rope ends into the dough to stick.

Continues

MAKES: *12 large pretzels*

PREP TIME: *2 hours*

COOK TIME: *15 minutes*

1½ cups (375 mL) warm water

1 package (¼ ounce/8 g) instant yeast

1 tablespoon (15 mL) raw honey

¾ teaspoon (4 mL) fine salt

4 cups (1 L) all-purpose flour, divided

⅓ cup (75 mL) unsalted butter, melted

1 cup (250 mL) finely grated old cheddar cheese, plus more for sprinkling

1 cup (250 mL) finely grated Asiago cheese, plus more for sprinkling

½ cup (125 mL) baking soda

1 egg, whisked, for egg wash

1 tablespoon (15 mL) coarse salt

7. Working in small batches and using a slotted spoon, add pretzels to the boiling water and boil for 30 seconds. Transfer to the prepared baking sheet, spacing them evenly.

8. Brush pretzels with the egg wash. Sprinkle with coarse salt and additional cheese, if desired.

9. Bake for 15 to 20 minutes, until golden brown. Let cool for 15 minutes on the baking sheet. Pretzels are best enjoyed within 24 hours. To extend shelf life, freeze in an airtight container or plastic bag for up to 2 weeks.

Sweet Potato and Chorizo Empanadas

When I think of an empanada, sweet potato is not the first ingredient that comes to mind. Here it's an unexpected but pleasant surprise, and it makes these empanadas a little pocket of fall. Adding to the sweetness of the potatoes, I've incorporated flavourful chorizo and warm notes from sage and cumin.

1. To make the Empanada Dough, in a large mixing bowl sift together the flour and salt. Add the butter and shortening. Using your hands or a pastry cutter, work in the butter and shortening until the mixture forms pea-sized crumbs. Work in the milk 1 tablespoon (15 mL) at a time until the dough begins to come together.

2. Turn the dough out onto a floured surface and shape it into a disc. Wrap in plastic wrap and refrigerate for at least 2 hours.

3. To make the Sweet Potato and Sausage Filling, in a large skillet heat the oil over medium heat. Add the sausage and cook, using a wooden spoon to break up the sausage into smaller pieces, until fully cooked and browned. Using a slotted spoon, transfer sausage to a small bowl.

4. To the fat in the pan, add the garlic, onion, sweet potato, sage, cumin, and salt and pepper to taste. Cook, stirring often, until the onion is translucent and the sweet potatoes are fork-tender, about 10 minutes. Return the sausage to the pan and cook for an additional minute. Remove from the heat and let cool to room temperature.

5. Preheat the oven to 350°F (180°C). Line a baking sheet with parchment paper.

6. On a heavily floured surface, roll out the chilled dough into a circle ¼ inch (5 mm) thick. Using a 4-inch (10 cm) cookie cutter, cut out 15 pastry rounds.

Continues

MAKES: *15 empanadas*

PREP TIME: *20 minutes*

COOK TIME: *35 minutes*

EMPANADA DOUGH

3 cups (750 mL) all-purpose flour

½ teaspoon (2 mL) fine salt

¾ cup (175 mL) unsalted butter, cold and cubed

⅓ cup (75 mL) shortening, cold and cubed

½ cup (125 mL) whole milk

1 egg, whisked, for egg wash

SWEET POTATO AND SAUSAGE FILLING

3 tablespoons (45 mL) extra-virgin olive oil

½ pound (225 g) fresh chorizo sausage, casings removed

2 cloves garlic, minced

1 medium onion, finely diced

1½ cups (375 mL) finely diced sweet potato

1 tablespoon (15 mL) roughly chopped fresh sage

2 teaspoons (10 mL) ground cumin

Salt and pepper

7. Spoon 1 tablespoon (15 mL) filling onto the centre of each round. Brush the edges with egg wash, fold each dough round in half and press together the edges to seal. Working your way from one end of the edge to the other, twist and curl down the dough, pinching together as you go. Brush the top with egg wash and transfer to the prepared baking sheet. Repeat with the remaining empanadas.

8. Bake for 20 to 25 minutes, until the dough is cooked through and the tops are golden brown. Serve warm.

BAKER'S NOTE Using a fork to seal and crimp the edges is a simpler way to create a designed edge.

Butternut Squash and Kale Strata

If you're looking for a delicious savoury fall breakfast dish, but don't want to wake up early to make it, look no further. This breakfast casserole—filled with layers of bread, eggs and cheese and flavoured with the season's squash and kale—is comforting and cozy and, best of all, can be prepped the night before. As in a stuffing or bread pudding, it's best to use day-old bread to help soak up the eggs and milk.

1. Preheat the oven to 375°F (190°C). Grease a 9- x 12-inch (3 L) baking dish.

2. In a large skillet over medium heat, combine the butter, olive oil, garlic and sage. Cook, stirring, until fragrant. Add the butternut squash and season with salt and pepper. Cook, stirring every few minutes, until the squash is fork-tender, about 10 minutes.

3. Stir in the kale and cook until wilted, about 2 minutes. Remove from the heat and let cool to room temperature.

4. In a medium mixing bowl whisk together the eggs, cheese, milk and cream. Season with salt and pepper.

5. In a large mixing bowl toss together the bread and the cooled squash mixture. Pour in the egg mixture and toss until the bread is fully coated and soaks up most of the egg mixture. Transfer to the prepared baking dish.

6. Bake for 45 to 50 minutes, until the bread is crispy and golden brown. Serve warm.

SERVES: *6 to 8*

PREP TIME: *15 minutes*

COOK TIME: *60 minutes*

2 tablespoons (30 mL) unsalted butter

2 tablespoons (30 mL) extra-virgin olive oil

2 cloves garlic, minced

1 tablespoon (15 mL) finely chopped fresh sage

1 small butternut squash (about 2 pounds/900 g), peeled and cut into ½-inch (1 cm) cubes

Salt and pepper

1 bunch kale, stemmed and roughly chopped

6 large eggs

2 cups (500 mL) grated old cheddar cheese

1 cup (250 mL) whole milk

½ cup (125 mL) heavy cream

1 loaf day-old sourdough bread, cut into ½-inch (1 cm) cubes

Sourdough, Chorizo and Wild Mushroom Stuffing

SERVES: *8 to 10*

PREP TIME: *30 minutes*

COOK TIME: *60 minutes*

4 tablespoons (60 mL) unsalted butter

1 pound (450 g) fresh chorizo sausage, casings removed

2 cloves garlic, minced

1 large white onion, chopped

3 stalks celery, chopped

3 cups (750 mL) sliced wild mushrooms (such as cremini, shiitake, chanterelle)

2 tablespoons (30 mL) chopped fresh sage

1 tablespoon (15 mL) chopped fresh thyme

Salt and pepper

1 loaf day-old sourdough bread, cut into ½-inch (1 cm) cubes

4 cups (1 L) low-sodium chicken stock

Stuffing is my favourite part of any holiday meal. In my family, the stuffing duty falls on me. (Okay, I insist on making it.) Over the years, I've branched out from a traditional white-bread-with-celery-and-onions stuffing and now love to incorporate sourdough, to add extra flavour, and different meats, such as sausage, which made this recipe an instant favourite. And to make holiday cooking that much easier, you can prepare this stuffing the day before and bake it right after you take the turkey out of the oven.

1. Preheat the oven to 375°F (190°C). Grease a 9- x 12-inch (3 L) baking dish.

2. In a large skillet over medium heat, melt the butter. Add the chorizo and cook, stirring from time to time, until the sausage has browned. Using a slotted spoon, transfer the chorizo to a bowl.

3. Add the garlic, onion, celery and mushrooms. Cook, stirring occasionally, until the vegetables have softened, about 10 minutes.

4. Return the chorizo to the pan and stir to combine. Add the sage, thyme, and salt and pepper to taste. Cook for an additional 2 minutes. Set aside to cool slightly.

5. In a large mixing bowl toss together the cubed bread, chorizo mixture and chicken stock. Season with additional salt and pepper.

6. Scrape into the prepared baking dish. Bake for 50 to 60 minutes, until the bread is crispy and golden brown. Serve warm.

BAKER'S NOTE It is always best to use day-old bread to help soak up the stock, but if that isn't an option, quickly toast the cubed bread in the oven for a couple of minutes to dry it out.

Roasted Butternut Squash Mac and Cheese

Mac and cheese is the ultimate comfort food. I have never met a single person who doesn't like it. This version incorporates roasted butternut squash, a fall staple in my books. The squash lightens the dish and adds a touch of natural creaminess. I prefer my mac and cheese loaded with cheese and topped with extra bread crumbs, and this recipe delivers! This will be a dish you return to all year round.

SERVES: *6 to 8*

PREP TIME: *20 minutes*

COOK TIME: *65 minutes*

2 cups (500 mL) peeled and ½-inch (1 cm) cubed butternut squash

2 tablespoons (30 mL) extra-virgin olive oil

Salt and pepper

1 pound (450 g) elbow macaroni

8 tablespoons (125 mL) unsalted butter, divided

¼ cup (60 mL) all-purpose flour

2 cloves garlic, grated

¼ teaspoon (1 mL) nutmeg

2 cups (500 mL) whole milk

1 cup (250 mL) heavy cream

2 bay leaves

2 cups (500 mL) grated aged cheddar cheese, divided

1½ cups (375 mL) grated Gruyère cheese

¾ cup (175 mL) panko breadcrumbs

1 teaspoon fresh thyme, roughly chopped

1. Preheat the oven to 350°F (180°C). Line a baking sheet with parchment paper.

2. On the prepared baking sheet, toss the squash with the oil and season with salt and pepper. Roast for 20 minutes, or until the squash is fork-tender. Remove from the oven. Increase the temperature to 375°F (190°C).

3. While the squash is roasting, bring a large pot of salted water to a boil and cook the macaroni until al dente. Drain and set aside.

4. In a large saucepan over low heat, melt 4 tablespoons (60 mL) of the butter. Add the flour and whisk constantly for 3 minutes. Add the garlic and nutmeg and cook, stirring, for an additional minute. Add the milk, cream and bay leaves. Season with salt and pepper. Simmer, stirring occasionally, over medium-low heat until the sauce thickens, about 10 minutes. Remove the bay leaves.

5. Add 1½ cups (375 mL) of the cheddar and the Gruyere and stir until melted. Add the cooked macaroni and roasted squash; stir to combine. Transfer to a 9- x 12-inch (3 L) baking dish.

6. For the breadcrumb topping, in a microwave-safe bowl, melt the remaining 4 tablespoons (60 mL) butter in the microwave. Stir in the panko and thyme. Sprinkle the remaining ½ cup (125 mL) cheddar evenly over the macaroni, followed by the panko mixture.

7. Bake for 30 minutes, or until the top is golden brown and the cheese is bubbling.

Scalloped Sweet Potatoes

1½ cups (375 mL) heavy cream

½ cup (125 mL) whole milk

2 bay leaves

2 or 3 sprigs fresh thyme

2 cloves garlic, minced

Salt and pepper

2½ pounds (1.125 kg) sweet potatoes, peeled and thinly sliced

2½ cups (625 mL) grated Gruyère cheese

3 teaspoons (15 mL) finely chopped fresh thyme

When Justin and I first met, he told me one of his favourite side dishes was scalloped potatoes—he used to buy the boxed version and eat the whole thing in one go. One night, I decided to surprise him with scalloped potatoes from scratch, and he never bought the store-bought version again. This dish is a sweet potato twist on the classic. The hint of sweetness from the sweet potatoes pairs so well with the thyme and Gruyère. Serve this at your next Thanksgiving; it's a delicious change from the classic sweet potato and marshmallow casserole.

1. In a small saucepan whisk together the cream, milk, bay leaves, thyme sprigs, garlic, and salt and pepper to taste. Bring to a gentle simmer over medium heat, then immediately remove from the heat. Let cool to room temperature. Discard the bay leaves and thyme sprigs.

2. Preheat the oven to 375°F (190°C). Grease a 9- x 12-inch (3 L) casserole dish.

3. Pour ¾ cup (175 mL) of the cream mixture into the casserole dish. Top with one-third of the sweet potatoes. Top evenly with ½ cup (125 mL) of the Gruyère and 1 teaspoon of the thyme. Season with salt and pepper. Repeat two more times, finishing with a generous layer of Gruyère and the remaining thyme.

4. Cover and bake for 15 minutes. Uncover and bake for an additional 35 to 40 minutes, until the potatoes are fork-tender and the cheese is golden brown on top. Serve immediately.

BAKER'S NOTE You can assemble the dish the day before, refrigerate it overnight and bake in a 375°F (190°C) oven an hour before serving time.

Turkey Cider Hot Dish

One of my favourite things about Thanksgiving is the leftover turkey. So many people end up throwing it away, but I enjoy creating new dishes from this holiday staple. I love this recipe's combination of turkey, apple cider, sweet potato, garlic and sage. The apple cider brings such an unexpected yet delicious sweetness to the dish. Considering the classic flavours at play here, you might just like this hot dish better than the actual holiday meal!

1. Preheat the oven to 350°F (180°C). Line a baking sheet with parchment paper.

2. Bake the tater tots on the prepared baking sheet for 15 minutes. (They will not be fully cooked.) Set aside. Keep the oven on while you prepare the filling.

3. In a deep 9-inch (23 cm) cast-iron skillet over medium-low heat, melt the butter. Add the garlic and stir until fragrant, about 30 seconds. Add the celery, onion, sweet potato, carrots and sage. Season with salt and pepper. Cook, stirring from time to time, until vegetables soften, about 10 minutes.

4. Sprinkle the cornstarch over the vegetables and stir to coat. Stir in the shredded turkey, followed by the apple cider and turkey stock. Bring to a simmer. Immediately remove from the heat. Stir in the cream and peas.

5. Arrange the tater tots over the filling. (I like to make a spiral shape.) Bake for 30 minutes, or until the tater tots are golden brown and the filling begins to bubble.

> **BAKER'S NOTE** I prefer to use dark meat in this recipe. It brings more moisture and flavour to the dish. If you don't have any leftover turkey, try it with chicken on a weeknight.

SERVES: *4 to 6*

PREP TIME: *15 minutes*

COOK TIME: *45 minutes*

1 pound (450 g) frozen tater tots

4 tablespoons (60 mL) unsalted butter

2 cloves garlic, minced

1½ cups (375 mL) diced celery

1½ cups (375 mL) diced onion

1½ cups (375 mL) peeled and diced sweet potato

1 cup (250 mL) peeled and diced carrots

2 tablespoons (30 mL) roughly chopped fresh sage

Salt and pepper

3 tablespoons (45 mL) cornstarch

2 cups (500 mL) shredded cooked turkey meat

1¼ cups (300 mL) sweet apple cider

2 cups (500 mL) turkey or chicken stock

¼ cup (60 mL) heavy cream

1 cup (250 mL) frozen peas

Roasted Brussels Sprout Gratin

SERVES: *10 to 12*

PREP TIME: *15 minutes*

COOK TIME: *50 minutes*

½ pound (225 g) pancetta, cubed

2 pounds (900 g) Brussels sprouts, trimmed and halved lengthwise

1 medium onion, thinly sliced

2 cloves garlic, minced

3 tablespoons (45 mL) extra-virgin olive oil

1 tablespoon (15 mL) quality balsamic vinegar

Salt and pepper

1½ cups (375 mL) grated aged white cheddar cheese

1 cup (250 mL) heavy cream

½ cup (125 mL) whole milk

1 cup (250 mL) panko breadcrumbs

2 tablespoons (30 mL) unsalted butter, melted

Despite my deep love of vegetables, I have to admit it took a while for Brussels sprouts to win me over. However, once I started roasting them with onions and bacon or pancetta, they revealed their true potential. And so this gratin was born. It is so flavourful and delicious. Cream and cheese may not make this the healthiest way to consume Brussels sprouts, but those who were once wary of this vegetable will find themselves asking for seconds (my dad included).

1. Preheat the oven to 350°F (180°C). Line a baking sheet with parchment paper and grease a 9- x 12-inch (3 L) baking dish.

2. In a skillet over medium heat, cook the pancetta until crispy, about 3 minutes. Remove from the pan and set aside.

3. In a large mixing bowl toss together the Brussels sprouts, onion, garlic, oil, balsamic vinegar, and salt and pepper to taste. Spread the mixture on the prepared baking sheet and roast for 15 minutes. Set aside to cool slightly. Keep the oven on.

4. In a large mixing bowl stir together the cheddar, cream and milk. Fold in the roasted Brussels sprouts mixture and pancetta. Pour the mixture into the prepared baking dish.

5. In a small bowl toss together the panko and butter. Evenly sprinkle over the filling. Bake for 35 to 40 minutes, until the top is golden brown and the sauce is bubbling. Serve immediately.

Winter

You would be hard pressed to find someone who loves winter as much as I do. The thought of waking up to a snow-covered yard puts the biggest smile on my face. Not to mention all the wool sweaters and blankets that finally get pulled out from the back of the closet. From cutting down a fresh Christmas tree to baking a month's worth of holiday cookies, including my Molasses Triple Ginger Cookies (page 181), winter is a season to celebrate. The fresh produce may be limited at this time of year, but this chapter focuses on comfort dishes, apples, cranberries, winter greens and winter spices.

Apples are great to bake with throughout the winter. Once the autumn is behind us, I pair them with familiar holiday flavours, like in the ultimate rustic dessert, my Apple Cranberry Brown Betty (page 198). I love playing with familiar winter and holiday flavours, which you'll notice in two of my favourite desserts: Eggnog Croissant Bread Pudding (page 202) and Vanilla Gingerbread Stout Cake (page 193). On the savoury side of things, this section focuses on hearty comfort dishes, such as Lentil Shepherd's Pie (page 222) and Cheesy Biscuit, Beef and Stout Pot Pie (page 217). These will warm you from the inside out on the coldest of winter days. A slow afternoon spent in the kitchen preparing something a little extra special for dinner is my favourite way to spend a snowy winter day.

Molasses Triple Ginger Cookies

These cookies are for all you ginger lovers. They are loaded with this zippy flavour in not two but three forms—ground, fresh and candied. I remember my first taste of candied ginger as a kid. I put a whole handful of it in my mouth and . . . well, you can imagine how that went over! But now I absolutely love using candied ginger in my baked goods (though I probably still wouldn't want a mouthful of it). These are the perfect winter cookie, with the sugared outside reminding me of a light dusting of snow. To warm you up on the snowiest and coldest of days, pair these with a hot cup of tea.

1. Preheat the oven to 375°F (190°C). Line a baking sheet with parchment paper.

2. In the bowl of a stand mixer fitted with the paddle attachment, cream the butter with the turbinado sugar until fluffy, about 2 minutes. Beat in the molasses. Beat in the egg, grated ginger and vanilla.

3. Sift in the flour, baking soda, ground ginger, cinnamon and salt. Beat until the dough comes together. Using a spatula, fold in the candied ginger.

4. Shape the dough into 1-inch balls and roll in the granulated sugar. Arrange the dough balls on the prepared baking sheet 2 inches (5 cm) apart and slightly flatten each ball.

5. Bake for 8 to 10 minutes, until the edges are lightly browned. Transfer to a rack to cool to room temperature. Store in an airtight container at room temperature for up to 2 days or in the freezer for up to 2 weeks.

> **BAKER'S NOTE** To get beautiful and dramatic cracks in the cookies, after 5 minutes in the oven, remove the cookies and gently push the dough down with the back of a spoon. Return to the oven and finish baking.

MAKES: *24 cookies*

PREP TIME: *10 minutes*

COOK TIME: *8 minutes*

¾ cup (175 mL) unsalted butter, room temperature

1 cup (250 mL) turbinado sugar

⅓ cup (75 mL) molasses

1 large egg

1 tablespoon (15 mL) grated fresh ginger

1 teaspoon (5 mL) pure vanilla extract

2½ cups (625 mL) all-purpose flour

2½ teaspoons (12 mL) baking soda

2 teaspoons (10 mL) ground ginger

½ teaspoon (2 mL) cinnamon

½ teaspoon (2 mL) fine salt

⅓ cup (75 mL) candied ginger, minced

Granulated sugar, for rolling

Salted Chocolate Chunk Cookies

MAKES: *24 cookies*

PREP TIME: *35 minutes*

COOK TIME: *8 minutes*

1¼ cups (300 mL) all-purpose flour

¼ cup (60 mL) buckwheat flour

¾ teaspoon (4 mL) fine salt

½ teaspoon (2 mL) baking soda

½ cup (125 mL) unsalted butter, softened

¾ cup (175 mL) packed light brown sugar

½ cup (125 mL) turbinado sugar

1 large egg

1 teaspoon (5 mL) pure vanilla extract

½ cup (125 mL) roughly chopped dark chocolate

½ cup (125 mL) roughly chopped milk chocolate

1 teaspoon (5 mL) flaky sea salt, for topping

As a baker, I've made chocolate chip cookies more times than I can count, so I can say with the utmost confidence, this is the ultimate chocolate chip cookie. It didn't take me long to realize I preferred my cookies with chunks of chocolate rather than chips. Then I discovered that mixing dark and milk chocolate gives the cookies the perfect level of sweetness. And after enough testing, I landed on the ideal proportion of sugar, butter and eggs to yield a thin cookie with a chewy centre and crispy edges. Adding a touch of buckwheat flour was my last improvement, and I haven't tried another recipe since! I like to make these cookies throughout the Christmas season, but in all honesty, it doesn't matter to me what month it is. These really are the one cookie I will never get tired of making or eating, and I think after one bite you'll feel the same way.

1. In a large mixing bowl sift together the all-purpose flour, buckwheat flour, salt and baking soda. Set aside.

2. In the bowl of a stand mixer fitted with the paddle attachment, beat together the butter, brown sugar and turbinado sugar until light and fluffy, about 2 minutes. Beat in the egg and vanilla. Gradually beat in the flour mixture, mixing until incorporated. Fold in the dark chocolate and milk chocolate. Refrigerate the dough for 30 minutes.

3. Preheat the oven to 350°F (180°C). Line 2 baking sheets with parchment paper.

4. Using an ice cream scoop, scoop out 2 tablespoons (30 mL) of cookie dough at a time and roll into a ball. Place no more than 12 cookies on each baking sheet, spacing them well apart. Press down to flatten and sprinkle with a pinch of flaky sea salt.

5. Bake for 8 to 10 minutes, until the edges are golden brown. Let cool on a rack to room temperature. Store in an airtight container at room temperature for up to 2 days or in the freezer for up to 2 weeks.

Winter Berry Granola

Homemade granola is a snack I always have on hand. It is so simple to whip up, and you can add just about any flavour you like. Granola works with a splash of almond milk, a bowl of yogurt or even unadorned, as a snack on its own. This hearty granola is perfect for the cold-weather season. Because winter produce is scarce, I've added dried blueberries, cranberries and raisins, and it all comes together with notes of citrus and maple syrup.

MAKES: *8 cups (2 L)*

PREP TIME: *10 minutes*

COOK TIME: *45 minutes*

3 cups (750 mL) old-fashioned rolled oats

4 ounces (115 g) quality dark chocolate, chopped

1 cup (250 mL) dried blueberries

1 cup (250 mL) dried cranberries

1 cup (250 mL) golden raisins

1 cup (250 mL) whole or slivered raw almonds

Grated zest of 1 orange

Pinch of cinnamon

Pinch of nutmeg

⅓ cup (75 mL) extra-virgin olive oil

⅓ cup (75 mL) pure maple syrup

2 tablespoons (30 mL) freshly squeezed orange juice

1 teaspoon (5 mL) pure vanilla extract

1. Preheat the oven to 325°F (160°C). Line a baking sheet with parchment paper.

2. In a large mixing bowl combine the oats, chocolate, blueberries, cranberries, raisins, almonds, orange zest, cinnamon and nutmeg. Stir until evenly mixed.

3. In a small bowl whisk together the oil, maple syrup, orange juice and vanilla. Pour over the oat mixture and toss until the granola is well coated.

4. Spread the granola on the prepared baking sheet. Bake for 45 minutes, stirring every 15 minutes, until golden brown and toasted. Let cool to room temperature on the baking sheet before transferring to an airtight container. Store at room temperature for up to 2 weeks.

Blood Orange Rosemary Cupcakes ———

MAKES: *12 cupcakes*

PREP TIME: *15 minutes*

COOK TIME: *20 minutes*

BLOOD ORANGE ROSEMARY CUPCAKES

1 tablespoon (15 mL) grated blood orange zest

1 tablespoon (15 mL) finely chopped fresh rosemary

1½ cups (375 mL) all-purpose flour

1 teaspoon (5 mL) baking powder

½ teaspoon (2 mL) fine salt

¼ teaspoon (1 mL) baking soda

½ cup (125 mL) unsalted butter, room temperature

¾ cup (175 mL) turbinado sugar

2 large eggs

2 tablespoons (30 mL) plain or vanilla full-fat yogurt

1 teaspoon (5 mL) pure vanilla extract

½ cup (125 mL) freshly squeezed blood orange juice

¼ cup (60 mL) whole milk

BLOOD ORANGE FROSTING

1 cup (250 mL) unsalted butter, room temperature

3 cups (750 mL) icing sugar

1 tablespoon (15 mL) grated blood orange zest

1 tablespoon (15 mL) freshly squeezed blood orange juice

1 teaspoon (5 mL) pure vanilla extract

Blood orange season begins in late December and lasts through the end of winter. Blood oranges have a gorgeous red flesh and a distinctive flavour, sweet and bitter at the same time. I love using their juice in my desserts (and cocktails too!). There is something about fresh rosemary that pairs so well with citrus fruit; together, they are the perfect mix of earthy and fresh. I hope you love these winter-inspired cupcakes as much as I do!

1. Preheat the oven to 325°F (160°C). Line a cupcake tin with 12 cupcake liners.

2. To make the Blood Orange Rosemary Cupcakes, in a medium mixing bowl stir together the orange zest, rosemary, flour, baking powder, salt and baking soda. Set aside.

3. In the bowl of a stand mixer fitted with the paddle attachment, cream the butter with the sugar until fluffy, about 2 minutes. Add the eggs, yogurt and vanilla. Beat until evenly mixed. Add the orange juice and milk and beat until incorporated. Add the dry ingredients and beat until the batter is smooth, about 2 minutes.

4. Evenly divide the batter among the cupcake liners. Bake for 20 minutes, until the tops bounce back when touched or a toothpick inserted in the centre comes out clean. Let cool on a rack while you prepare the frosting.

5. To make the Blood Orange Frosting, in the bowl of a stand mixer fitted with the paddle attachment, cream the butter with the sugar until fluffy, about 8 minutes. Add the orange zest, orange juice and vanilla. Beat for an additional 60 seconds.

6. Transfer the frosting to a large pastry bag fitted with a large open star tip. Holding the bag vertically above a cupcake, squeeze while moving in a circular motion. Once you reach the top, stop squeezing and gently lift off. Repeat for the remaining cupcakes.

Peppermint Bark Blondies

Every December I look forward to indulging in a tin of peppermint bark. A roommate in university introduced me to this Christmas goody, and since then it's been a seasonal must! Aside from eating this addictive treat straight from the tin, I like to incorporate the three flavours—white chocolate, dark chocolate and peppermint—into other winter baked goods. These blondies are like a soft, chewy version of the classic bark. I've incorporated the peppermint into the blondies only, but if you are a huge fan of this flavour, try adding a little peppermint extract to the ganache too.

1. Preheat the oven to 350°F (180°C). Grease an 8-inch (20 cm) square baking dish.

2. To make the Dark Chocolate Peppermint Blondies, in a large mixing bowl combine the eggs, sugar, butter, molasses, vanilla and peppermint extract. Beat until smooth.

3. Sift in the flour, salt and baking powder. Beat until well combined, about 2 minutes. Fold in the dark chocolate chunks.

4. Scrape the batter into the prepared baking dish. Bake for 25 to 30 minutes, until the edges have browned and the centre is slightly soft. Transfer to a rack and let cool completely in the pan.

5. To make the White Chocolate Ganache, in a medium microwave-safe bowl combine the white chocolate and cream. Melt in the microwave in 30-second increments, stirring after each increment, until fully melted. Let cool for 5 minutes.

6. Remove blondies from the pan. Spread the ganache evenly over the top and sprinkle with the crushed candy canes. Refrigerate for 30 minutes before slicing.

MAKES: *16 blondies*

PREP TIME: *15 minutes*

COOK TIME: *30 minutes*

DARK CHOCOLATE PEPPERMINT BLONDIES

2 large eggs

2 cups (500 mL) turbinado sugar

1 cup (250 mL) unsalted butter, melted

2 tablespoons (30 mL) molasses

2 teaspoons (10 mL) pure vanilla extract

2 teaspoons (10 mL) peppermint extract

2 cups (500 mL) all-purpose flour

1 teaspoon (5 mL) fine salt

½ teaspoon (2 mL) baking powder

6 ounces (170 g) quality dark chocolate, roughly chopped

½ cup (125 mL) crushed candy canes, for topping

WHITE CHOCOLATE GANACHE

8 ounces (225 g) quality white chocolate, roughly chopped

2 tablespoons (30 mL) heavy cream

White Chocolate Gingerbread Biscotti

My family is as Italian as they come. Although my culinary style may not always reflect my upbringing, I had to include my grandparents' favourite treat: biscotti! In their house, every meal was followed by an espresso and Italian cookie for dipping (even if you were only eight years old). These gingerbread biscotti are the perfect festive treat for dipping in your winter espresso, spiced latte or any warming beverage. Packed with gingerbread flavour and candied ginger, and drizzled with white chocolate, these make a great edible gift to give family and friends over the holiday season.

1. Line a baking sheet with parchment paper.

2. In a large mixing bowl cream together the butter, ¾ cup (175 mL) of the sugar and the molasses until fluffy, about 2 minutes. Add the eggs one at a time, beating after each addition, then beat in the vanilla.

3. In a separate large mixing bowl sift the flour, baking powder, salt, ginger, cinnamon, nutmeg, cloves and pepper. Gradually add the dry ingredients to the wet ingredients, mixing on low speed until the dough comes together. Fold in the candied ginger.

4. Turn the dough out onto the prepared baking sheet. Shape into a loaf 16 inches (40 cm) long and 3 inches (8 cm) wide. Brush with the egg white and sprinkle with the remaining 1 tablespoon (15 mL) sugar. Let chill in the refrigerator or freezer for 30 minutes.

5. Preheat the oven to 350°F (180°C).

6. Bake the loaf for 25 to 30 minutes, until pale golden. Let the loaf cool slightly on the baking sheet, about 10 minutes. (Keep the oven on.) Cut the loaf into 1-inch (2.5 cm) thick slices.

7. Arrange the slices cut side down on the baking sheet and bake for an additional 5 minutes on each side, or until golden. Transfer to racks and let cool to room temperature.

Continues

MAKES: *12 biscotti*

PREP TIME: *15 minutes*

COOK TIME: *35 minutes*

½ cup (125 mL) unsalted butter, room temperature

¾ cup (175 mL) + 1 tablespoon (15 mL) turbinado sugar, divided

2 tablespoons (30 mL) molasses

3 large eggs

1 teaspoon (5 mL) pure vanilla extract

2 cups (500 mL) all-purpose flour

2 teaspoons (10 mL) baking powder

½ teaspoon (2 mL) fine salt

2 teaspoons (10 mL) ground ginger

1 teaspoon (5 mL) cinnamon

½ teaspoon (2 mL) nutmeg

½ teaspoon (2 mL) ground cloves

½ teaspoon (2 mL) freshly ground black peppercorns

½ cup (125 mL) candied ginger, finely chopped

1 large egg white, whisked

4 ounces (115 g) quality white chocolate, roughly chopped

8. While the biscotti are cooling, in a small microwave-safe bowl melt the white chocolate in the microwave in 30-second increments, stirring after each increment, until fully melted. Drizzle biscotti with the melted chocolate. Store in an airtight container at room temperature for up to 1 week or in the freezer for up to a month.

Vanilla Gingerbread Stout Cake

This cake is the ultimate holiday cake. Not only is it a showstopper but it also contains everything you want in festive flavour. The stout keeps the cake extra moist and really accentuates the gingerbread spices. The sugared cranberries are as beautiful as any edible garnish, and as a bonus, they taste good! I love topping all sorts of cupcakes, cakes and cheesecakes over the holidays with these sugared cranberries.

1. Preheat the oven to 325°F (160°C). Grease three 8-inch (20 cm) round cake pans and line the bottom of each pan with parchment paper.

2. To make the Gingerbread Stout Cake, in a large mixing bowl sift together the flour, baking soda, salt, ginger, cinnamon, cloves, nutmeg and pepper. Set aside.

3. In the bowl of a stand mixer fitted with the paddle attachment, cream together the butter, oil and sugar until fluffy, about 2 minutes. Add the eggs one at a time, beating after each addition and scraping down the sides of the bowl before the next addition. Add the molasses and vanilla and beat until smooth.

4. Stir in the flour mixture alternately with the dark stout, making 1/3 additions of flour mixture and 1/3 additions of stout, mixing until fully incorporated before each addition. Once all the ingredients have been added, beat for an additional 60 seconds.

5. Evenly divide the batter among the prepared cake pans. Bake for 25 to 30 minutes, until the centres bounce back when touched or a toothpick inserted in the centre comes out clean. Transfer to racks and let cool completely before removing the cakes from the pans.

6. While the cakes are cooling, make the Sugared Cranberries. In a small saucepan over medium heat, combine ½ cup (125 mL) of the sugar and the water. Stir until the sugar dissolves. Add the cranberries and stir to coat. Spread on a rack set over a baking sheet and let sit for 1 hour or until dry. In a large mixing bowl toss the cranberries with the remaining 1 cup (250 mL) sugar. Spread on the rack and let sit for an additional hour.

Continues

SERVES: *8 to 10*

PREP TIME: *2 hours*

COOK TIME: *25 minutes*

GINGERBREAD STOUT CAKE

4 cups (1 L) all-purpose flour

3½ teaspoons (17 mL) baking soda

1 teaspoon (5 mL) fine salt

1 tablespoon (15 mL) ground ginger

2 teaspoons (10 mL) cinnamon

1 teaspoon (5 mL) ground cloves

½ teaspoon (2 mL) nutmeg

¼ teaspoon (1 mL) pepper

¾ cup (175 mL) unsalted butter, room temperature

¼ cup (60 mL) canola oil

2½ cups (625 mL) turbinado sugar

6 large eggs

¾ cup (175 mL) molasses

2 teaspoons (10 mL) pure vanilla extract

2 cups (500 mL) stout beer, such as Guinness

SUGARED CRANBERRIES

½ cup (125 mL) + 1 cup (250 mL) white sugar, divided

½ cup (125 mL) water

4 cups (1 L) fresh cranberries

TO FINISH

1 batch Vanilla Buttercream (page 238)

7. Using a long serrated knife, level the top of each cake, if necessary. Place 1 cake layer trimmed side up on a cake stand or cake turntable and dollop approximately ¾ cup (175 mL) Vanilla Buttercream onto the middle. Using an offset spatula, smooth the frosting flat, spreading it to the edges. Place a second cake layer on top and gently press down to stabilize it. Spread another ¾ cup (175 mL) frosting over the top and smooth flat. Top with the final layer of cake and gently press down to stabilize and level it. Dollop 2 cups (500 mL) frosting onto the top and use the offset spatula to gently work the frosting evenly over the top and down the sides. Be sure to coat every inch of the cake with frosting.

8. For a "naked" finish, hold the edge of the offset spatula or a bench scraper against the cake and slowly turn the cake, scraping away the frosting to expose the layers of cake. Wipe the edge of the spatula clean of frosting as you go. This will result in a beautiful naked cake.

9. Before serving, top the cake with the Sugared Cranberries, stacking them higher in the centre. Store in the refrigerator uncovered for up to 24 hours or until ready to serve.

White Chocolate Matcha Cheesecake

SERVES: *10 to 12*

PREP TIME: *15 minutes*

COOK TIME: *90 minutes*

GRAHAM CRACKER CRUST

2 cups (500 mL) graham cracker crumbs

½ cup (125 mL) granulated sugar

½ cup (125 mL) unsalted butter, melted

¼ teaspoon (1 mL) fine salt

WHITE CHOCOLATE CHEESECAKE FILLING

4 packages (8 ounces/225 g each) full-fat cream cheese, room temperature

1½ cups (375 mL) granulated sugar

2 tablespoons (30 mL) all-purpose flour, sifted

2 tablespoons (30 mL) pure matcha powder, sifted

4 large eggs, room temperature

2 large egg yolks, room temperature

1 teaspoon (5 mL) pure vanilla extract

2 ounces (55 g) quality white chocolate, melted and slightly cooled

WHITE CHOCOLATE GANACHE

1 cup (250 mL) crème fraîche

4 ounces (115 g) quality white chocolate, melted and cooled

1 teaspoon (5 mL) pure vanilla extract

Every Christmas I prepare a cheesecake for dessert. I guess you could say I am "famous" in my family for my cheesecakes. Each year I like to make a different one, introducing my family to some unexpected flavours. When my white chocolate matcha (powdered green tea) cake became a huge success on my blog, I knew these flavours had to be incorporated into a cheesecake—this one, to be exact. Cheesecakes can be quite fussy to bake properly, which is probably why so many of us resist making our own. Follow these directions and you will never again fear making one at home. Using all room-temperature ingredients is a very important first step to a successful cheesecake.

1. Preheat the oven to 450°F (230°C).

2. To make the Graham Cracker Crust, in a medium mixing bowl combine the graham cracker crumbs, sugar, butter and salt. Stir until evenly combined. Pour the mixture into a 9-inch (23 cm) springform pan and press evenly and firmly over the bottom and 1 inch (2.5 cm) up the sides of the pan. Refrigerate the crust while you prepare the filling.

3. To make the White Chocolate Cheesecake Filling, in the bowl of a stand mixer fitted with the paddle attachment combine the cream cheese, sugar, flour and matcha powder. Beat until smooth. Add the eggs and egg yolks one at a time, beating after each addition and scraping down the edges of the bowl before adding the next. Add the vanilla and beat for an additional 30 seconds, until the filling is silky smooth. Fold in the white chocolate.

4. Pour the filling over the chilled graham crust. Bake for 15 minutes, then lower the heat to 225°F (110°C) and bake for an additional 45 to 50 minutes, until the centre is almost set. Turn the oven off and let the cheesecake sit in the oven for 20 minutes while the temperature gradually cools.

5. Remove the sides of the pan and let the cheesecake rest at room temperature for 1 hour. Cover and refrigerate overnight.

6. Before serving, make the White Chocolate Ganache. Whisk together the crème fraîche, white chocolate and vanilla. Spread an even layer of the ganache over the cheesecake.

BAKER'S NOTE This is the perfect dessert to make a day or two in advance. Just be sure to add the ganache right before serving time!

Apple Cranberry Brown Betty

SERVES: *6 to 8*

PREP TIME: *20 minutes*

COOK TIME: *60 minutes*

APPLE CRANBERRY FILLING

6 to 8 medium apples, peeled, cored and thinly sliced

1½ cups (375 mL) fresh cranberries

½ cup (125 mL) turbinado sugar

1 teaspoon (5 mL) pure vanilla extract

½ cup (125 mL) sweet apple cider, divided

SPICED BISCUIT CRUMBS

1½ cups (375 mL) all-purpose flour

⅔ cup (150 mL) turbinado sugar

1 teaspoon (5 mL) baking soda

½ teaspoon (2 mL) fine salt

½ teaspoon (2 mL) cinnamon

¼ teaspoon (1 mL) nutmeg

¼ teaspoon (1 mL) ground cloves

¾ cup (175 mL) unsalted butter, cold and cubed

FOR SERVING

Vanilla ice cream or Fresh Whipped Cream (page 240)

I am always going on about how much I like the topping of a crumble or crisp. I am that person whose serving is 75% (okay, 90%) topping. When I discovered brown Bettys they quickly became my new best friend. They are very similar to a crisp or crumble, except the crumble mixture and fruit are layered throughout the dish, like a lasagna. It is traditional to use breadcrumbs, but here I go the extra mile and use a spiced biscuit crumb mixture. I also top each layer with a splash of fresh apple cider because . . . well, I don't think we need a reason to use apple cider! And fresh cranberries turn this dessert into a holiday must-have.

1. Preheat the oven to 350°F (180°C). Butter a 9-inch (23 cm) round baking dish.

2. To make the Apple Cranberry Filling, in a large mixing bowl toss together the apples, cranberries, sugar and vanilla. Set aside.

3. To make the Spiced Biscuit Crumbs, in a separate large mixing bowl sift the flour, sugar, baking soda, salt, cinnamon, nutmeg and cloves. Add the butter. Using your hands or a pastry cutter, work in the butter until the mixture forms pea-sized crumbs.

4. Evenly spread one-third of the Apple Cranberry Filling in the prepared baking dish. Top with one-third of the Spiced Biscuit Crumbs, spreading in an even layer. Evenly pour over ¼ cup (60 mL) of the apple cider. Repeat the layers two more times, finishing with a layer of the crumb mixture. Do not pour cider over the top layer.

5. Bake for 60 minutes, or until the top is golden brown and the fruit filling is bubbling. Serve warm with ice cream or whipped cream.

Brown Butter Sticky Pudding

Sticky pudding is one of my all-time favourite desserts. A sweet, dense cake soaked in a decadent caramel sauce—what's not to love! I've amplified the classic recipe by featuring a brown butter toffee sauce here, which adds an extra level of flavour with its toasty, nutty notes. I serve this straight out of the pan, drizzled with a touch more sauce and a dollop of whipped cream.

1. Preheat the oven to 350°F (180°C). Grease a 9- x 12-inch (3 L) baking dish.

2. To make the cake, in a small bowl pour the boiling water over the dates. Let stand for 10 minutes to allow the dates to soften.

3. Transfer the dates and the water to a blender and purée until smooth. Set aside until ready to use.

4. In a large mixing bowl cream the butter with the sugar until fluffy, about 2 minutes. Add the eggs, one at a time, beating after each addition. Beat in the vanilla and puréed dates until well incorporated, about 2 minutes. Sift in the flour, baking powder, baking soda and salt. Beat until the batter is smooth.

5. Scrape the batter into the prepared baking dish. Bake for 20 minutes, or until the top bounces back when touched or a toothpick inserted in the centre comes out clean.

6. While the cake is baking, prepare the Brown Butter Toffee Sauce. In a medium skillet over medium heat, melt the butter. Swirling the pan occasionally, cook until the butter turns a toasty brown colour. When you begin to smell a nutty aroma, pour it into a bowl to cool slightly, about 5 minutes.

7. Return the butter to the pan and add the sugar, cream and salt. Cook over medium heat, constantly stirring, until the sugar is fully dissolved. Remove from the heat and stir in the vanilla.

8. Once the cake is finished baking, immediately poke holes in the top using a knife and pour three-quarters of the Brown Butter Toffee Sauce over it. Let stand for 10 minutes before serving. Serve with vanilla ice cream or whipped cream, drizzled with the remaining sauce.

SERVES: *8*

PREP TIME: *10 minutes*

COOK TIME: *35 minutes*

CAKE

1 cup (250 mL) Medjool dates, pitted

¾ cup (175 mL) water, boiled

½ cup (125 mL) unsalted butter, room temperature

1 cup (250 mL) turbinado sugar

2 large eggs, room temperature

2 teaspoons (10 mL) pure vanilla extract

1½ cups (375 mL) all-purpose flour

1 teaspoon (5 mL) baking powder

1 teaspoon (5 mL) baking soda

¼ teaspoon (1 mL) fine salt

BROWN BUTTER TOFFEE SAUCE

¾ cup (175 mL) unsalted butter

1½ cups (375 mL) packed light brown sugar

¾ cup (175 mL) heavy cream

¼ teaspoon (1 mL) fine salt

1 teaspoon (5 mL) pure vanilla extract

FOR SERVING

Vanilla ice cream or Fresh Whipped Cream (page 240)

Eggnog Croissant Bread Pudding

SERVES: *6 to 8*

PREP TIME: *15 minutes*

COOK TIME: *55 minutes*

EGGNOG CROISSANT BREAD PUDDING

5 large eggs

1½ cups (375 mL) packed light brown sugar

2½ cups (625 mL) eggnog

½ cup (125 mL) heavy cream

2 tablespoons (30 mL) quality bourbon

1 teaspoon (5 mL) pure vanilla extract

¼ teaspoon (1 mL) nutmeg

¼ teaspoon (1 mL) fine salt

8 day-old croissants, torn into 1-inch (2.5 cm) pieces

BOURBON CARAMEL SAUCE

1 cup (250 mL) granulated sugar

⅓ cup (75 mL) water

¼ cup (60 mL) heavy cream

4 tablespoons (60 mL) unsalted butter

1 tablespoon (15 mL) quality bourbon

¼ teaspoon (1 mL) fine salt

Eggnog: you either love it or you hate it. I think this recipe makes it obvious which side of the fence I stand on. For me, it's just not the holidays without eggnog, and I love baking with it at this time of the year. This bread pudding is so delicious. The croissants give it an extra richness you just don't get from plain old bread. Day-old works best, as it really helps soak up that eggnog goodness. Don't be shy with the caramel sauce, either!

1. Preheat the oven to 350°F (180°C). Grease a 9- x 12-inch (3 L) baking dish.

2. To make the Bread Pudding, in a large mixing bowl combine the eggs, brown sugar, eggnog, cream, bourbon, vanilla, nutmeg and salt. Whisk until blended. Add the croissant pieces and toss to coat.

3. Pour the pudding mixture into the prepared baking dish. Bake for 50 to 60 minutes, until the top is golden brown. Let rest for 15 minutes before serving.

4. While the pudding bakes, make the Bourbon Caramel Sauce. In a small saucepan combine the sugar and water. Heat over medium heat. Do not stir, as it will result in a crystallized mess. Heat until the sugar dissolves and the mixture is a deep amber colour, 5 to 8 minutes. Remove from the heat and immediately whisk in the cream, butter, bourbon and salt. Let cool to room temperature. The sauce will thicken as it cools.

5. As soon as you remove the bread pudding from the oven, pour ½ cup (125 mL) of the caramel sauce evenly over it. Serve the pudding warm with additional Bourbon Caramel Sauce drizzled over top.

Maple Sugar Pie Tartlets

In high school French class, we all had to give a presentation on a French-Canadian dish. Naturally, I focused on cheese, but someone else chose sugar pie. Having never heard of this dish, I was instantly intrigued. One bite and I was hooked! (I can't tell you how many "samples" I ate that day.) This recipe is a more refined version of the high school treat I so enjoyed, and if you want to take it one step further, substitute maple sugar for the brown sugar.

1. Preheat the oven to 350°F (180°C).

2. On a lightly floured surface, roll out the pie dough until ¼ inch (5 mm) thick. Using a pastry wheel or knife, cut out eight 4-inch (10 cm) rounds. Transfer the rounds to eight 3-inch (8 cm) tartlet pans, pressing into the bottom and sides. Trim the edges. Place the pastry shells on a baking sheet and freeze while you prepare the filling.

3. In a large mixing bowl combine the eggs, cream, sugar, maple syrup, flour, vanilla and salt. Whisk until smooth.

4. Carefully divide the filling among the tartlet shells. Drop 2 or 3 cubes of butter into each tartlet. Bake for 25 to 35 minutes, until the edges are golden brown and the centres jiggle slightly. Let set for 2 hours in the refrigerator. Serve with a dollop of whipped cream.

MAKES: *eight 3-inch (8 cm) tartlets*

PREP TIME: *15 minutes*

COOK TIME: *25 minutes*

1 batch Single Pie Dough (page 243), chilled

2 large eggs

1½ cups (375 mL) heavy cream

1 cup (250 mL) packed light brown sugar

1 cup (250 mL) pure maple syrup

¼ cup (60 mL) all-purpose flour

1 teaspoon (5 mL) pure vanilla extract

½ teaspoon (2 mL) fine salt

4 tablespoons (60 mL) unsalted butter, finely diced

Fresh Whipped Cream (page 240), for serving

Salted Bourbon Pecan Pie

SERVES: *6 to 8*

PREP TIME: *15 minutes*

COOK TIME: *50 minutes*

1 batch Single Pie Dough (page 243), chilled

3 large eggs

1 cup (250 mL) packed light brown sugar

¾ cup (175 mL) golden corn syrup

⅓ cup (75 mL) unsalted butter, melted

2 tablespoons (30 mL) quality bourbon

1 teaspoon (5 mL) pure vanilla extract

½ teaspoon (2 mL) fine salt

1½ cups (375 mL) pecan halves

¼ teaspoon (1 mL) coarse salt

I wouldn't say no to any type of pie served during the holiday season, but pumpkin, apple and pecan are always at the top of my list. There is something so festive about these pies that one bite instantly puts me in a celebratory mood. (Although, truthfully, as a Christmas enthusiast, it doesn't take much to get me excited about the holidays.) This salted bourbon pecan pie is like a butter tart on steroids. It has the perfect hint of bourbon flavour, crunch from the pecans, and a touch of salt to offset the sweetness.

1. Preheat the oven to 350°F (180°C).

2. On a lightly floured surface, roll out the pie dough until ¼ inch (5 mm) thick. Gently lift and transfer the dough to a 9-inch (23 cm) pie plate, pressing the dough into the bottom and sides of the plate. Trim the edges, leaving a 1-inch (2.5 cm) overhang. Fold under the overhang, then crimp the edges. To crimp the edges, place an index finger on the lip of the pie plate and pinch around that finger with the index finger and thumb of your other hand, holding the dough in between. Refrigerate while you prepare the filling.

3. In a medium mixing bowl combine the eggs, sugar, corn syrup, butter, bourbon, vanilla and fine salt. Whisk until smooth.

4. Evenly scatter the pecans over the bottom of the pie shell. Pour the filling over the pecans. Sprinkle the top evenly with the coarse salt.

5. Bake for 25 minutes, then tent with foil and bake for an additional 25 minutes, or until the crust is golden brown and the centre jiggles only slightly. If after the cooking time the pie jiggles too much, bake in additional 5-minute increments. Transfer to a rack and allow the pie to set at room temperature for 4 hours before serving.

Winter Pear and Smoked Gorgonzola Pizza

This is not your average pizza recipe; I guess you could say it is a cross between a white pizza and a flatbread. I use honey-caramelized onions as the base to pair with the smoky, bold Gorgonzola cheese. Although regular Gorgonzola will work, I recommend tracking down the smoked variety—it just might become your favourite cheese! I like to call the Comice pear the "Christmas" pear, as it begins to appear at the market in the early winter just in time for holiday fruit platters and cheese boards. In this pizza, the sweetness from the honey and pears pairs perfectly with the salty smokiness of the Gorgonzola.

1. Make the Pizza Dough and let it rise until doubled in size, about 1 hour.

2. While the dough rises, in a large skillet combine the butter, onions, and salt and pepper to taste. Cook over medium-low heat, stirring every few minutes, until the onions are caramelized, about 25 minutes. Turn the heat up to medium and add the honey. Toss until the onions are browned, about 5 minutes. Set aside until ready to use.

3. Preheat the oven to 425°F (220°C), with a pizza stone if using.

4. Once the dough has risen, on a lightly floured surface, roll it out until ¼ inch (5 mm) thick. Brush each side with olive oil and season with salt and pepper. Transfer the dough to a baking sheet or the hot pizza stone.

5. Top with the caramelized onions, followed by the mozzarella, Gorgonzola, pear, walnuts and thyme. Bake for 15 to 20 minutes, until the crust is golden and the cheese is bubbling. Garnish with additional thyme and serve immediately.

BAKER'S NOTE If you are unable to find Comice pears, substitute a Bosc or Anjou pear.

SERVES: *4 to 6*

PREP TIME: *60 minutes*

COOK TIME: *45 minutes*

1 batch Pizza Dough (page 118)

4 tablespoons (60 mL) unsalted butter

2 large onions, thinly sliced

Salt and pepper

1 tablespoon (15 mL) quality honey

2 tablespoons (30 mL) extra-virgin olive oil

1½ cups (375 mL) grated mozzarella cheese

½ cup (125 mL) crumbled smoked Gorgonzola cheese

1 Comice pear, cored and thinly sliced

¼ cup (60 mL) roughly chopped walnuts

1 teaspoon (5 mL) roughly chopped fresh thyme, plus more for garnish

No-Knead Bacon, Cheddar and Herb Bread

SERVES: *8 to 10*

PREP TIME: *12 hours*

COOK TIME: *45 minutes*

3½ cups (875 mL) all-purpose flour

1 cup (250 mL) whole wheat flour

2 teaspoons (10 mL) sea salt

1¼ teaspoons (6 mL) instant dry yeast

2½ cups (625 mL) warm water

1 pound (450 g) strip bacon

1 clove garlic, grated

1½ cups (375 mL) grated aged cheddar cheese

1 tablespoon (15 mL) roughly chopped fresh rosemary

1 tablespoon (15 mL) roughly chopped fresh thyme

1½ teaspoons (7 mL) roughly chopped fresh sage

1 tablespoon (15 mL) extra-virgin olive oil

1 teaspoon (5 mL) coarse salt

¼ teaspoon (1 mL) pepper

This is my winter take on no-knead bread. It is so hearty, filled with bacon, cheese and wintery herbs. Baking this bread in a Dutch oven gives it a soft, chewy interior and an extra-crispy crust. If you're looking for a bread to dip into your favourite winter soups and stews, look no further!

1. In a large mixing bowl combine the all-purpose flour, whole wheat flour, salt and yeast. Stir until combined. Pour in the warm water and stir until a sticky dough forms. Tightly cover the bowl with plastic wrap and let the dough rest at room temperature until doubled in size, about 12 hours.

2. Preheat the oven to 400°F (200°C). Line a baking sheet with foil.

3. Place the bacon strips side by side on the prepared baking sheet and cook for 15 minutes, or until crispy around the edges. Let cool to room temperature. Transfer bacon to a cutting board and finely chop. Set aside until ready to use.

4. Once the dough has doubled in size, stir in the bacon, garlic, cheddar, rosemary, thyme and sage. Turn the dough out onto a heavily floured surface and knead to work in the fillings.

5. Shape the dough into a round loaf. Brush with the oil and sprinkle with the salt and pepper. Cover with a damp tea towel and let rest for 30 minutes while you preheat the oven.

6. Place a lidded 4-quart (3.8 L) Dutch oven in the oven and preheat the oven to 450°F (230°C).

7. Once the oven is preheated, remove the Dutch oven and quickly flour the bottom and sides. Lift the round loaf and drop it inside. Place the lid on the Dutch oven and bake for 25 minutes. Remove the lid and bake for an additional 20 minutes, or until the top is golden brown and crispy. Remove from the pot and let cool slightly before slicing.

Roasted Garlic and Cheese Pull-Apart Bread

True story: the first time Justin and I made this bread, the two of us devoured the entire loaf within an hour. It is that good! I already had trouble resisting "normal" garlic bread, so when I swapped out plain old white bread for sourdough and packed it with loads of cheese and roasted garlic, I knew this pull-apart bread wouldn't last long. This works great as a party appetizer; guests tend to gather around and pull off one cube at a time. I like serving this for Super Bowl parties too. I'm not a football fan, but recipes like this make it easy to get through four hours of football . . . or at least make it to halftime. Bonus points if you serve this alongside some hearty winter chili.

1. Preheat the oven to 400°F (200°C).

2. Slice the top off of the head of garlic to expose the cloves and drizzle with olive oil. Wrap tightly in foil, place directly on the oven rack and roast until very soft, 45 to 60 minutes. Unwrap and let cool before squeezing the cloves from their skins.

3. In a small skillet over medium heat, melt the butter. Mash in the roasted garlic and red chili flakes, if using. Season with salt and pepper. Remove from the heat.

4. Without cutting all the way to the bottom, cut the sourdough loaf into 1-inch (2.5 cm) slices. Turn the loaf 90 degrees and cut the bread the same way, again making sure not to cut all the way through.

5. Pour the melted butter mixture all over the top and into the slices, trying to reach every nook and cranny. Stuff with the mozzarella and Parmesan.

6. Transfer the bread to a 10-inch (25 cm) oven-safe skillet or a baking sheet. Bake for 25 to 30 minutes, until the loaf is golden brown and the cheese is melted. Sprinkle with the parsley and serve immediately.

BAKER'S NOTE This recipe is so simple to whip up and can be prepared hours before baking. Simply wrap it tightly in foil, then unwrap it when ready to bake.

SERVES: *6 to 8*

PREP TIME: *15 minutes*

COOK TIME: *70 minutes*

1 head garlic

2 tablespoons (30 mL) extra-virgin olive oil

½ cup (125 mL) unsalted butter, melted

½ teaspoon (2 mL) red chili flakes (optional)

Salt and pepper

1 loaf sourdough bread

1½ cups (375 mL) grated mozzarella cheese

1 cup (250 mL) freshly grated Parmesan cheese

1 tablespoon (15 mL) chopped fresh parsley

Salted Honey Challah

I started making bread from scratch in my university years. What began with the simple no-knead variety quickly escalated into more intricate loaves, such as this braided challah. Bread baking is one of my favourite things to do throughout the winter, on those days when it is just too cold to step outside. This egg-based bread offers a hint of sweetness. It is beautifully braided and can be enjoyed alongside a morning cup of coffee. It also makes for the most decadent French toast and bread pudding. Because I love my sweet and salty pairings, I flavour this challah with honey and sprinkle the top with coarse sea salt. If you wanted to switch things up, you could replace the honey with an equal amount of pure maple syrup.

1. To make the Challah, in the bowl of a stand mixer, whisk together the water and sugar. Sprinkle over the yeast and let stand for 5 minutes to allow the yeast to activate. If bubbles do not form on the top, start over with fresh yeast.

2. Fit the mixer with the dough hook and add the eggs, egg yolk, honey and oil. Mix on low speed until evenly incorporated. With the mixer on low speed, add the flour 1 cup (250 mL) at a time, gradually increasing to medium speed. Add the fine salt with the last 1½ cups (375 mL) flour. Knead on medium speed until a smooth dough forms, about 5 minutes.

3. On a lightly floured surface, shape the dough into a ball. Place back in the mixer bowl, cover with a damp tea towel and let rest at room temperature until doubled in size, about 2 hours.

4. While the dough rises, prepare the Honey Egg Wash. In a small bowl whisk together the egg yolk, honey and water. Set aside until ready to use.

5. Preheat the oven to 375°F (190°C). Line a baking sheet with parchment paper.

Continues

MAKES: *1 loaf*

PREP TIME: *2 hours*

COOK TIME: *35 minutes*

CHALLAH

1 cup (250 mL) lukewarm water

1 teaspoon (5 mL) granulated sugar

2¼ teaspoons (11 mL) instant yeast

2 large eggs

1 large egg yolk

¼ cup (60 mL) quality honey

¼ cup (60 mL) canola oil

4½ cups (1.125 L) all-purpose flour

2 teaspoons (10 mL) fine salt

HONEY EGG WASH

1 large egg yolk, beaten

1 tablespoon (15 mL) quality honey

1 teaspoon (5 mL) water

1 teaspoon (5 mL) coarse sea salt

6. Once the dough has risen, divide it into three equal pieces. Roll each piece into a rope roughly 16 inches (40 cm) long and 1½ inches (4 cm) thick. Place the ropes next to each other on the prepared baking sheet. Pinch the ropes together at one end and braid the ropes as you would braid hair. Pinch together the other ends and tuck both ends under. Brush with the Honey Egg Wash. Cover with a damp tea towel and let rise at room temperature for an additional hour.

7. Brush again with the egg wash and sprinkle with the coarse salt. Bake for 35 to 40 minutes, until golden. Transfer to a rack and let cool slightly before slicing.

Cheesy Biscuit, Beef and Stout Pot Pie

Saying that my dad "loves" Guinness is an understatement. Being Italian, we are a wine-drinking household, but Guinness is the one (and only) beer my dad keeps on hand. Every time we go out for dinner, instead of wine he orders a dark stout with his meal. Because of him, I began experimenting with its distinctive bold flavour in my own kitchen. This pot pie is for my dad and for anyone who loves stout as much as they love a hearty stew. This isn't your traditional pot pie, however, as it's topped with buttery, flaky, cheesy biscuits. This dish will warm you from the inside out when the thermometer drops below zero. My dad gave this dish a double thumbs-up, so I know you're going to love it too.

1. To make the Cheesy Biscuit Topping, in a large mixing bowl sift together the flour, baking powder and salt. Add the cubed butter and work it in with your hands or a pastry cutter until the mixture forms pea-sized crumbs. Mix in the cheese, followed by the milk, and knead just until the dough comes together.

2. Shape the dough into a disc, wrap in plastic wrap and refrigerate while you prepare the Pot Pie Filling.

3. Preheat the oven to 375°F (190°C).

4. In a large skillet over medium heat, heat the olive oil. Once the oil is hot, sear the stewing beef, working in batches, about 30 seconds per side. (The beef does not need to be cooked through at this stage.) Using a slotted spoon, transfer the beef to a bowl.

5. Add the garlic to the skillet and stir until fragrant, about 30 seconds. Add the onion, celery, carrots, parsnips and potatoes. Cook, stirring occasionally, for 10 minutes or until the onions begin to turn translucent. Add the mushrooms, rosemary, thyme, and salt and pepper to taste. Cook, stirring occasionally, for an additional 5 minutes.

6. Pour in the beer and beef stock. Return the browned beef and any juices to the pan. Bring to a boil, then reduce heat and simmer for 10 minutes.

Continues

SERVES: *6 to 8*

PREP TIME: *30 minutes*

COOK TIME: *60 minutes*

CHEESY BISCUIT TOPPING

3 cups (750 mL) all-purpose flour

3½ teaspoons (17 mL) baking powder

1½ teaspoons (7 mL) fine salt

¾ cup (175 mL) unsalted butter, cold and cubed

2 cups (500 mL) grated old white cheddar cheese

1¼ cups (300 mL) whole milk

1 tablespoon (15 mL) heavy cream

POT PIE FILLING

¼ cup (60 mL) extra-virgin olive oil

2 pounds (900 g) stewing beef

2 cloves garlic, minced

1 medium onion, diced

3 stalks celery, diced

2 medium carrots, peeled and diced

2 medium parsnips, peeled and diced

2 medium Yukon Gold potatoes, diced

2 cups (500 mL) thinly sliced cremini mushrooms

2 tablespoons (30 mL) finely chopped fresh rosemary

2 tablespoons (30 mL) finely chopped fresh thyme

Salt and pepper

1½ cups (375 mL) stout beer, such as Guinness

2½ cups (625 mL) low-sodium beef stock

2 tablespoons (30 mL) cornstarch

1 cup (250 mL) frozen peas

7. In a small bowl whisk the cornstarch into ¼ cup (60 mL) of the simmering beef broth. Pour the mixture back into the pan, stir well, then add the frozen peas. Cook until the filling thickens. Transfer to a 9- x 12-inch (3 L) baking dish.

8. On a lightly floured surface, roll out the biscuit dough until ¾ inch (2 cm) thick. Cut out 8 rounds with a 2½-inch (6 cm) cookie cutter. Arrange the rounds over the filling. Brush each biscuit with the cream.

9. Bake for 40 minutes, or until the biscuit topping is golden and the filling is bubbling. Serve immediately.

Winter Greens Frittata

By New Year's Day, I feel sick at the sight of a holiday dish or dessert (at least for a few days). This winter greens frittata has the comfort of a winter dish, but with a lightness you will crave after festive celebrations. The frittata is like a baked omelet, but better. I find myself sneaking to the fridge to pick at the leftovers of this dish. Bonus: if you're like me and you struggle with flipping omelettes (almost always ending up with scrambled eggs), a frittata doesn't require flipping! Feel free to use whatever variety of winter greens you have on hand—kale, chard, collard greens, rapini—the options are endless.

1. Preheat the oven to 350°F (180°C). Grease an 8-inch (20 cm) square baking dish or an 8-inch (20 cm) cast-iron skillet.

2. In a large saucepan over medium heat, melt the butter. Add the oil, garlic, rosemary, thyme and sage and cook, stirring, until fragrant, 30 seconds to 1 minute. Add the onion and cook, stirring from time to time, until softened and turning translucent, about 5 minutes.

3. Stir in the winter greens and cook until they are fully wilted, about 2 minutes. Season with salt and pepper. Remove from the heat and let cool to room temperature.

4. In a large mixing bowl whisk together the eggs and milk until foamy. Stir in the Parmesan, Swiss cheese, panko and the cooled greens mixture.

5. Pour into the prepared baking dish and bake for 20 to 25 minutes, until the top is golden and puffed. Let stand for 5 minutes before serving.

SERVES: *4 to 6*

PREP TIME: *15 minutes*

COOK TIME: *30 minutes*

2 tablespoons (30 mL) unsalted butter

2 tablespoons (30 mL) extra-virgin olive oil

1 clove garlic, minced

1 tablespoon (15 mL) roughly chopped fresh rosemary

1 tablespoon (15 mL) roughly chopped fresh thyme

1½ teaspoons (7 mL) roughly chopped fresh sage

1 medium onion, chopped

6 cups (1.5 L) packed stemmed and roughly chopped winter greens

Salt and pepper

6 large eggs

2 tablespoons (30 mL) whole milk

1 cup (250 mL) freshly grated Parmesan cheese

1 cup (250 mL) grated Swiss cheese

½ cup (125 mL) panko breadcrumbs

Lentil Shepherd's Pie

SERVES: *8 to 10*

PREP TIME: *20 minutes*

COOK TIME: *75 minutes*

MASHED POTATO TOPPING

2 pounds (900 g) medium Yukon gold potatoes, quartered

½ cup (125 mL) grated Gouda cheese

½ cup (125 mL) heavy cream

4 tablespoons (60 mL) unsalted butter

1 teaspoon (5 mL) finely chopped fresh thyme

Salt and pepper

LENTIL FILLING

4 tablespoons (60 mL) unsalted butter

1 onion, chopped

2 cloves garlic, minced

1 stalk celery, chopped

1 carrot, peeled and chopped

1 tablespoon (15 mL) roughly chopped fresh thyme

1 tablespoon (15 mL) all-purpose flour

1 tablespoon (15 mL) tomato paste

¾ cup (175 mL) vegetable or chicken stock

½ cup (125 mL) dry white wine

½ cup (125 mL) frozen peas

2 cups (500 mL) cooked or canned lentils

Shepherd's pie is a dish my mom often made for a typical weekday dinner. Not exactly something you would expect from an Italian family, but it was definitely a household favourite. When my sister became a vegetarian, I wanted to create a shepherd's pie she would love. However, for Italians, a meatless meal is practically a sacrilege. I knew the dish would have to satisfy vegetarians and non-vegetarians alike, which is how I landed on lentils; they are the perfect substitute for ground beef. Just as hearty, they soak up so much flavour. My sister loves cheese more than anyone I know, so I added freshly grated Gouda to the mashed potato topping. I promise, this dish will be a hit even if you are a meat lover!

1. Preheat the oven to 350°F (180°C).

2. To make the Mashed Potato Topping, place the potatoes in a large pot and cover with cold water. Bring to a boil and cook until the potatoes are fork-tender, about 15 minutes.

3. Drain the potatoes, return to the pot, and immediately add the cheese, cream, butter and thyme. Mash until smooth. Season with salt and pepper. Set aside while you prepare the filling.

4. To make the Lentil Filling, heat a large skillet over medium heat. Melt the butter, then add the onion and garlic and cook, stirring, until fragrant, about 2 minutes. Add the celery, carrot and thyme. Cook, stirring often, until the vegetables soften, about 10 minutes.

5. Stir in the flour, then stir in the tomato paste. Add the stock, wine and frozen peas. Bring to a simmer. Stir in the lentils and cook for an additional 5 minutes.

6. Transfer the filling to a 9- x 12-inch (3 L) baking dish. Spoon the Mashed Potato Topping onto the filling, and using the back of a spoon, spread the potatoes evenly over the filling. Bake for 45 to 50 minutes, until the filling is bubbling and the potatoes are golden. Let stand for 5 minutes before serving.

Winter Greens Galette

SERVES: *4 to 6*

PREP TIME: *15 minutes*

COOK TIME: *40 minutes*

GALETTE DOUGH

1¼ cups (300 mL) all-purpose flour

¼ cup (60 mL) whole wheat flour

1 large clove garlic, grated

1 teaspoon (5 mL) finely chopped
fresh rosemary

1 teaspoon (5 mL) salt

¼ teaspoon (1 mL) freshly ground
black pepper

½ cup (125 mL) unsalted butter,
cold and cubed

¼ cup (60 mL) ice water

WINTER GREENS FILLING

2 tablespoons (30 mL) unsalted
butter

2 tablespoons (30 mL) extra-virgin
olive oil

1 medium white onion, finely
chopped

1 clove garlic, minced

1 tablespoon (15 mL) finely
chopped fresh rosemary

Salt and pepper

2 tablespoons (30 mL) all-purpose
flour

8 cups (2 L) stemmed and roughly
chopped mixed winter greens
(such as collards, rapini, chard
and kale)

½ cup (125 mL) + 1 tablespoon
(15 mL) heavy cream, divided

½ cup (125 mL) grated Fontina
cheese

½ cup (125 mL) grated Gouda
cheese

1 teaspoon (5 mL) coarse salt
(optional)

When I was testing this recipe, Justin gave it 100 out of 10. With a
score like that, I had no doubt this galette was going to make the book.
This dish is a cross between a gratin and a pie. It has the perfect balance of greens and creaminess—comfort feels with the healthiness
of vegetables. I've packed in even more flavour by adding a touch of
whole wheat flour, rosemary and garlic to the dough.

1. To make the Galette Dough, in a large mixing bowl combine the all-purpose flour, whole wheat flour, garlic, rosemary, salt and pepper. Stir
well. Add the butter and work into the dough using your hands until
the mixture forms pea-sized crumbs. Add the ice water 1 tablespoon
(15 mL) at a time and toss until the dough comes together.

2. Turn the dough out onto a lightly floured surface and shape into
a disc. Wrap in plastic wrap and refrigerate for at least 2 hours or
overnight.

3. To make the Winter Greens Filling, in a large saucepan over
medium heat, melt the butter with the oil. Add the onion, garlic,
rosemary, and salt and pepper to taste. Cook, stirring often, until the
onions soften and turn translucent, about 5 minutes.

4. Sprinkle in the flour and stir well. Stir in the greens and cook
until they have fully wilted. Remove from the heat and stir in ½ cup
(75 mL) of the cream, the Fontina and Gouda. Let cool slightly while
you roll out the dough.

5. Preheat the oven to 375°F (190°C). Line a baking sheet with parchment paper.

6. On a lightly floured surface, roll out the dough into a 12-inch (30 cm)
square. The dough should be ¼ inch (5 mm) thick. Transfer the dough
to the prepared baking sheet. Scrape the cooled filling onto the dough
and smooth flat, leaving a 1-inch (2.5 cm) border. Fold over the edges,
pressing the corners together. Brush the dough with the reamining
1 tablespoon (15 mL) cream and sprinkle with coarse salt, if desired.
Refrigerate for 15 minutes.

7. Bake for 25 to 30 minutes, until the filling is bubbling and the crust
is golden. Let rest for 5 minutes before serving.

Root Vegetable Crumble

This is the perfect side dish for any winter meal, be it a Sunday-night dinner, a holiday gathering or a potluck. Hearty and warming, it's loaded with an array of root vegetables and topped with a flavourful herb crumble. This recipe was inspired by my sister; as a vegetarian, she always pushes me to rethink how to make recipes more vegetable-forward, and this crumble is the perfect example!

1. Preheat the oven to 350°F (180°C).

2. To make the Root Vegetable Filling, in a small saucepan combine the olive oil, garlic and onion. Cook over medium heat, stirring often, until the onion begins to turn translucent, about 5 minutes. Stir in the rosemary, thyme, and salt and pepper to taste. Set aside.

3. In a large mixing bowl toss together the beet, sweet potato, turnip, carrot, celery root and rutabaga. Add the onion mixture, Gruyère, vegetable stock, cream and milk. Stir well. Season with salt and pepper. Transfer to a 9- x 12-inch (3 L) baking dish.

4. To make the Herb Crumble, in a medium mixing bowl combine the panko, walnuts, rosemary, thyme and olive oil. Toss until well mixed. Season with salt and pepper. Evenly sprinkle the crumble topping over the vegetables.

5. Bake for 90 minutes, or until the vegetables are fork-tender and the filling is bubbling. Serve immediately.

SERVES: *8 to 10*

PREP TIME: *20 minutes*

COOK TIME: *90 minutes*

ROOT VEGETABLE FILLING

¼ cup (60 mL) extra-virgin olive oil

2 cloves garlic, minced

1 large onion, diced

1 tablespoon (15 mL) finely chopped fresh rosemary

1 tablespoon (15 mL) finely chopped fresh thyme

Salt and pepper

1 beet, peeled and cubed

1 medium sweet potato, peeled and cubed

1 turnip, cubed

1 carrot, peeled and diced

½ medium celery root, peeled and cubed

½ medium rutabaga, peeled and cubed

2 cups (500 mL) grated Gruyère cheese

1½ cups (375 mL) low-sodium vegetable stock

1¼ cups (300 mL) heavy cream

¾ cup (175 mL) whole milk

HERB CRUMBLE

2 cups (500 mL) panko breadcrumbs

½ cup (125 mL) walnuts, finely chopped

1 teaspoon (5 mL) finely chopped fresh rosemary

1 teaspoon (5 mL) finely chopped fresh thyme

¼ cup (60 mL) extra-virgin olive oil

Salt and pepper

Rosemary Cheddar Popovers

MAKES: *12 popovers*

PREP TIME: *35 minutes*

COOK TIME: *25 minutes*

2 large eggs, room temperature

1 cup (250 mL) all-purpose flour

1 cup (250 mL) whole milk

2 tablespoons (30 mL) unsalted
   butter, melted

2 tablespoons (30 mL) finely
   chopped fresh rosemary

¾ teaspoon (4 mL) fine salt

½ cup (125 mL) grated old
   cheddar cheese

Similar to Yorkshire pudding, popovers are an eggy, airy pastry, almost what I imagine biting into a cloud would be like. They are called popovers because they "pop" over the pan while they bake. They are the perfect snack or bread to serve alongside a winter stew. I use a mini popover pan for this recipe, but a standard muffin pan will do the trick. Mix these up throughout the seasons by adding different herbs and cheeses.

1. In a large mixing bowl whisk the eggs until light and frothy. Add the flour, milk, butter, rosemary and salt. Whisk until smooth. Let the batter rest at room temperature for 30 minutes.

2. While the batter is resting, preheat the oven to 450°F (230°C). Grease and flour a 12-mould mini popover pan.

3. Pour the batter into the moulds, filling a quarter full. Divide the cheese among the moulds, then top with additional batter until three-quarters full.

4. Bake for 15 minutes, then lower oven temperature to 350°F (180°C) and bake for an additional 10 minutes, or until the popovers have doubled in size and are golden brown. Remove popovers from pan and let cool for about 5 minutes before serving. Popovers are best enjoyed within 24 hours.

Wild Mushroom and Coffee Dutch Baby

When the holidays are over, even I crave savoury comfort foods over sweets. While we often associate a breakfast Dutch baby with maple syrup and fresh fruit toppings, I've taken a less traditional approach here. This savoury, thyme-scented Dutch baby is filled with coffee-braised wild mushrooms and is topped with a fried egg. It may sound like an odd pairing, but coffee really helps bring the flavours of the mushrooms and chicken stock together. I recommend using a bold roast for the best flavour. Brew yourself an extra cup to sip on as you prepare this dish. It's the perfect hearty winter breakfast for two.

1. Place an 8-inch (20 cm) cast-iron skillet on the top rack of the oven and preheat the oven to 450°F (230°C).

2. In a blender, pulse the eggs until frothy. Add the flour, milk, thyme, salt and pepper. Blend until smooth. Let rest for at least 15 minutes while the oven heats.

3. Once the oven is heated, remove the skillet and add the butter. Carefully swirl the melting butter to coat the pan's edges. Immediately pour in the batter and place back in the oven. Bake for 20 minutes, or until the Dutch baby is puffed and golden brown around the edges. Do not open the oven during this time or the Dutch baby will not rise properly.

4. While the Thyme Dutch Baby bakes, prepare the Mushroom Topping. In a large skillet over medium heat, melt the butter. Add the mushrooms, garlic, shallot, thyme, and salt and pepper to taste. Cook, stirring often, until the mushrooms have softened, 5 to 7 minutes. Stir in the stock and coffee. Simmer until the liquid is reduced by half.

5. Shortly before the Dutch baby is done, prepare the sunny-side-up egg. Grease a small nonstick skillet and heat over medium heat. Crack in the egg and cook until the white sets and the yolk begins to thicken slightly, about 3 minutes.

6. Pour the Mushroom Topping over the Dutch baby and top with the sunny-side-up egg. Serve immediately.

SERVES: 2

PREP TIME: *30 minutes*

COOK TIME: *20 minutes*

THYME DUTCH BABY

3 large eggs, room temperature

⅔ cup (150 mL) all-purpose flour

⅔ cup (150 mL) whole milk, room temperature

½ teaspoon (2 mL) finely chopped fresh thyme

¼ teaspoon (1 mL) fine salt

¼ teaspoon (1 mL) pepper

4 tablespoons (60 mL) unsalted butter

MUSHROOM TOPPING

2 tablespoons (30 mL) unsalted butter

2 cups (500 mL) wild mushrooms (such as enoki and chanterelle), torn if large

1 clove garlic, minced

1 shallot, minced

½ teaspoon (2 mL) finely chopped fresh thyme

Salt and pepper

¾ cup (175 mL) low-sodium chicken stock

½ cup (125 mL) strong brewed coffee

1 large egg

Kale, Bacon and Parmesan Bread Pudding

SERVES: *4 to 6*

PREP TIME: *15 minutes*

COOK TIME: *45 minutes*

1 pound (450 g) strip bacon, roughly chopped

2 cloves garlic, minced

1 medium onion, chopped

Salt and pepper

1 bunch kale, stemmed and torn

5 large eggs

1½ cups (375 mL) whole milk

1 cup (250 mL) heavy cream

8 cups (2 L) day-old white bread, small cubes

2 cups (500 mL) freshly grated Parmesan cheese

This bread pudding is similar to a breakfast strata, but the extra milk makes the filling moist and less eggy. I keep the seasonings to a minimum because the bacon, kale and Parmesan bring bold flavours of their own. When I think of winter comfort food, this is a dish I crave! It is perfect at a Sunday winter brunch, as either a main or a side dish.

1. Preheat the oven to 350°F (180°C). Grease six 8-ounce (250 mL) ramekins or a 9- x 12-inch (3 L) baking dish.

2. In a large skillet over medium heat, cook the bacon, stirring occasionally, until crispy, about 5 minutes. Using a slotted spoon, remove the bacon from the pan and set aside.

3. Add the garlic and onion to the pan and season with salt and pepper. Cook, stirring from time to time, until the onion softens and turns translucent. Add the kale and toss until fully wilted. Remove from the heat and let the mixture cool for about 10 minutes.

4. In a large mixing bowl whisk together the eggs, milk and cream. Stir in the bread, then stir in the Parmesan and the kale mixture. Season with salt and pepper.

5. Divide evenly among the prepared ramekins or scrape into the baking dish. Bake ramekins for 30 to 35 minutes or the baking dish for 40 to 45 minutes, until the top is golden. Let rest for 5 minutes before serving.

Rosemary and Sea Salt Baked Nuts

I love gifting something edible over the holiday season, and baked nuts are the perfect choice. These rosemary-infused nuts have a much longer shelf life than cookies (another popular gift) and can be enjoyed all winter long. You can use any assortment of nuts you have on hand, but I like to include equal parts pecans, walnuts, cashews, peanuts and almonds. The variety presents beautifully and makes for a great addition to any charcuterie board.

1. Preheat the oven to 350°F (180°C). Line a baking sheet with parchment paper.

2. Add the nuts to a large mixing bowl. In a small bowl whisk together the sugar, maple syrup, butter, rosemary, salt, chili flakes and black pepper. Pour the mixture over the nuts and toss well to coat.

3. Spread the nuts on the prepared baking sheet. Bake for 30 minutes, stirring every 10 minutes, or until the nuts are toasted and caramelized.

4. Let cool completely on the baking sheet. Store in jars at room temperature for up to 2 weeks.

MAKES: *3 cups*

PREP TIME: *10 minutes*

COOK TIME: *30 minutes*

3 cups (750 mL) assorted unsalted, unroasted nuts (pecans, walnuts, cashews, peanuts, almonds)

¼ cup (60 mL) packed light brown sugar

¼ cup (60 mL) pure maple syrup

4 tablespoons (60 mL) unsalted butter, melted

2 tablespoons (30 mL) finely chopped fresh rosemary

1½ teaspoons (7 mL) flaky sea salt

1 teaspoon (5 mL) red chili flakes

½ teaspoon (2 mL) black pepper

Baking Basics

Behind every great recipe, there's a perfect base recipe. From frostings to dough to caramel, this section features all the staple recipes I use throughout *Bake the Seasons*. Everything is better when it is made from scratch, so I always recommend using simple, quality ingredients when possible, instead of items like prepared pizza dough, frozen pie shells and store-bought caramel sauce. I encourage you to try your hand at these basics when baking up one of my seasonal dishes, as well as integrating them into your regular culinary routine.

Vanilla Buttercream

MAKES: *4 cups (1 L)*

PREP TIME: *10 minutes*

2 cups (500 mL) unsalted butter, room temperature

3 to 4 cups (750 mL to 1 L) icing sugar, to taste

2 teaspoons (10 mL) pure vanilla extract

Pinch of fine salt

When it comes to cake, I am a vanilla over chocolate kind of girl. This is my go-to vanilla buttercream recipe for frosting all my cakes and cupcakes. It also happens to serve as a great base for all sorts of flavoured buttercreams, so I often add different extracts and spices to switch up the flavour. Be sure to use room-temperature butter, as it whips better than cold butter. Also, use the paddle attachment on your stand mixer; the whisk attachment can create unwanted bubbles when frosting.

1. In the bowl of a stand mixer fitted with the paddle attachment, cream the butter with the sugar until fluffy, about 8 minutes.

2. Add the vanilla and salt. Beat for an additional 60 seconds.

3. Frost cakes and cupcakes as desired. This frosting is best used fresh.

Chocolate Buttercream

MAKES: *4 cups (1 L)*

PREP TIME: *10 minutes*

2 cups (500 mL) unsalted butter, room temperature

½ cup (125 mL) cocoa powder

3 to 4 cups (750 mL to 1 L) icing sugar, to taste

2 tablespoons (30 mL) heavy cream

1 teaspoon (5 mL) pure vanilla extract

Pinch of fine salt

This is my go-to chocolate frosting. It is rich and creamy like all chocolate buttercreams should be, and totally fuss-free, as it uses cocoa powder instead of melted chocolate. The splash of cream at the end helps lighten the buttercream, making it easier to frost your favourite cakes and cupcakes.

1. In the bowl of a stand mixer fitted with the paddle attachment, cream the butter, cocoa powder and sugar until fluffy, about 8 minutes.

2. Add the cream, vanilla and salt. Beat for an additional 60 seconds.

3. Frost cakes and cupcakes as desired. This frosting is best used fresh.

Cream Cheese Frosting

This is the frosting my sisters request no matter what type of cake I am making. (I could slather it on cardboard and they would be satisfied!) I use this frosting for my Zucchini Pineapple Snack Cake (page 71) and Hummingbird Cupcakes (page 17), but it works well with a simple chocolate cake too. The trick is to thoroughly cream the butter and sugar first, so when it comes time to add the cream cheese, the sugar is already well dispersed throughout the butter. Cold cream cheese works best, as it makes for a much firmer frosting, which is easier to decorate with and pipe. Be careful not to overmix the frosting once the cream cheese has been added, or the frosting can turn runny.

MAKES: *4 cups (1 L)*

PREP TIME: *10 minutes*

1 cup (250 mL) unsalted butter, room temperature

4 cups (1 L) icing sugar, or to taste

1 teaspoon (5 mL) pure vanilla extract

Pinch of fine salt

16 ounces (450 g) full-fat cream cheese, cold and cubed

1. In the bowl of a stand mixer fitted with the paddle attachment, cream the butter with the sugar until fluffy, about 8 minutes.

2. Add the vanilla and salt. Beat for an additional 30 seconds.

3. With the mixer on low speed, beat in the cream cheese 2 ounces (55 g) at a time, beating until incorporated before adding more. Once all the cream cheese has been added, turn the mixer to high speed and beat for an additional 30 seconds.

4. Frost cakes and cupcakes immediately after preparing. This frosting is best used fresh.

Fresh Whipped Cream

MAKES: *2 cups (500 mL)*

PREP TIME: *5 minutes*

1 cup (250 mL) heavy cream, cold

2 tablespoons (30 mL) granulated sugar

1 teaspoon (5 mL) pure vanilla extract

Fresh whipped cream is the perfect garnish for so many of the sweets in this book, such as Peaches and Cream Waffles (page 96) and Rhubarb Upside-Down Cake (page 22). Personally, I almost always serve my desserts with this whipped cream rather than ice cream. It's simple to whip up and tastes ten times better than that store-bought stuff. I always make this by hand, using a mixing bowl and a whisk. I find it fascinating to watch as the cream transforms from a liquid into fluffy clouds.

1. Place a mixing bowl in the freezer for 15 minutes. This will help keep the whipped cream cold.

2. Add the cream to the bowl and whisk to soft peaks, about 3 minutes. Add the sugar and vanilla. Whisk to stiff peaks, about 1 minute. Refrigerate for up to 4 hours.

Vanilla Simple Syrup

MAKES: *1 cup (250 mL)*

PREP TIME: *2 minutes*

COOK TIME: *5 minutes*

1 cup (250 mL) granulated sugar

1 cup (250 mL) water

1 teaspoon (5 mL) pure vanilla extract

Often used in drinks and canning, simple syrup finds its way into baking too. If I am making a cake a day in advance, I like to brush each layer with simple syrup before frosting to ensure the cake stays moist. I also find this syrup essential when making any type of cake or shortcake. Sometimes I add fresh herbs to transform it to a rosemary simple syrup or thyme simple syrup. Use this as the base for endless possibilities!

1. In a small saucepan combine the sugar and water. Bring to a boil over medium heat, stirring until the sugar fully dissolves.

2. Remove from the heat and stir in the vanilla. Let cool to room temperature.

3. Store in a glass jar in the refrigerator for up to 1 month.

Salted Caramel Sauce

Salted caramel sauce is one of my favourite things to incorporate into desserts. I love all things sweet and salty, so this hits the spot every time. Aside from baking with salted caramel, this sauce can be enjoyed drizzled over ice cream and drinks, my personal favourite being a salted caramel apple cider in the fall. When making this, just be sure to keep a close eye on the sugar as it turns from clear to deep amber, as it can burn very quickly!

1. In a saucepan over medium heat, combine the sugar and water. Do not stir. Bring to a boil and let cook, without stirring, until the mixture turns deep amber, about 5 to 7 minutes.

2. Remove from the heat and immediately whisk in the cream, butter and salt.

3. Transfer to a glass jar and let cool to room temperature. Store in the refrigerator for up to 2 weeks. To bring the caramel back to room temperature, microwave in 30-second increments.

MAKES: *2 cups (500 mL)*

PREP TIME: *5 minutes*

COOK TIME: *5 minutes*

1 cup (250 mL) granulated sugar

⅓ cup (75 mL) water

¾ cup (175 mL) heavy cream

4 tablespoons (60 mL) unsalted butter, room temperature

1 teaspoon (5 mL) sea salt

Single Pie Dough

This is my go-to basic pie dough. I like using a mix of butter and shortening, to benefit from the flavour of the butter and the flakiness that shortening provides. It's the best of both worlds! Use this recipe for pies that do not require a top layer of crust.

1. In a large mixing bowl stir together the flour and salt. Add the butter and shortening. Using your hands or a pastry cutter, work in the butter and shortening until the mixture forms pea-sized crumbs. Add the water 1 tablespoon (15 mL) at a time, tossing until the dough begins to come together.

2. Turn the dough out onto a floured surface and shape into a disc. Wrap in plastic wrap and refrigerate for at least 2 hours. Use within 2 days or freeze for up to 2 weeks. Thaw in the fridge the day before using.

MAKES: *1 single-crust pie shell*

PREP TIME: *10 minutes*

1½ cups (375 mL) all-purpose flour, sifted

¼ teaspoon (1 mL) fine salt

⅓ cup (75 mL) unsalted butter, cold and cubed

3 tablespoons (45 mL) shortening, cold

¼ cup (60 mL) ice water

Double Pie Dough

This is my go-to crust, doubled to make both a bottom and top crust for a pie. It is a very easy dough to braid and shape with.

1. In a large mixing bowl stir together the flour and salt. Add the butter and shortening. Using your hands or a pastry cutter, work in the butter and shortening until the mixture forms pea-sized crumbs. Add the water 1 tablespoon (15 mL) at a time, tossing until the dough begins to come together.

2. Turn the dough out onto a floured surface and shape into 2 discs. Wrap each in plastic wrap and refrigerate for at least 2 hours. Use within 2 days or freeze for up to 2 weeks. Thaw in the fridge the day before using.

MAKES: *1 double-crust pie shell*

PREP TIME: *10 minutes*

3 cups (750 mL) all-purpose flour, sifted

½ teaspoon (2 mL) fine salt

¾ cup (175 mL) unsalted butter, cold and cubed

⅓ cup (75 mL) shortening, cold

½ cup (125 mL) ice water

Acknowledgments

Ever since I first began *Modest Marce*, I have had nothing but support from my family and friends. Without them, I wouldn't be sitting here, writing the final sentences of my first cookbook. My adventures over the past few years have taught me that hard work really does pay off. If you are passionate about something, go for it! As my favourite lyricist, James Mercer, wrote, "Remember what they say, there's no shortcut to a dream. It's all blood and sweat, and life is what you manage in between."

Thank you to my editor, Rachel Brown, and the entire team at Penguin Random House Canada for believing in my talent and vision. I couldn't be more grateful to work with you on my first book. What started out as the most exciting email of 2017 turned into one of my most rewarding adventures.

Thank you to Bob's Red Mill and Ghirardelli for making quality ingredients and providing me with everything I needed to test my recipes countless times. Thank you to Staub Canada for supporting me since day one and donating the beautiful cookware to help me make this book happen.

To my grandparents, the four angels watching over me and everything I do. I know this book would make you so proud. I wish you were here to see everything unfold. You taught me the importance of hard work and determination.

To my sister Adrianna, for helping me start my photography adventure and getting me to where I am today. For being the creative and successful older sister to always look up to. For reminding me that my photography is good, even when I'm being extra hard on myself.

To my sister Sabrina. Not only did you put up with sharing a room with me for our entire childhood, but you continued to put up with me when I followed you to university. Those endless nights of baking in your dorm kitchen when I should have been studying are my favourite university memories. For always editing the grammar in my blog posts (and texts), even when not asked. You are the greatest sister anyone could have.

To my mom and dad, no words could ever be enough to thank you for everything you have done for me. You have helped me every step of the way, with the cooking, cleaning and taste testing. You are truly the world's best parents. Many girls fear they will grow up and become their mothers; I couldn't be prouder to have done so.

To Justin, the Jeffrey to my Ina. I am the luckiest person to get to call you my partner. My blog and this book would not have happened without you. You constantly push me to be the best I can be and always support me in everything I do. You never let me give up, no matter how many times I wanted to. Like we always say, don't let the bastards get you down! I love you.

Index